P9-EED-124

At Issue

Civil Disobedience

Other Books in the At Issue Series

At Issue

| Civil Disobedience

Elizabeth Schmermund, Book Editor

GREENHAVEN
PUBLISHING

Published in 2018 by Greenhaven Publishing, LLC
353 3rd Avenue, Suite 255, New York, NY 10010

Copyright © 2018 by Greenhaven Publishing, LLC

First Edition

All rights reserved. No part of this book may be reproduced in any form
without permission in writing from the publisher, except by a reviewer.

Articles in Greenhaven Publishing anthologies are often edited for length to meet page
requirements. In addition, original titles of these works are changed to clearly present
the main thesis and to explicitly indicate the author's opinion. Every effort is made to
ensure that Greenhaven Publishing accurately reflects the original intent of the authors.
Every effort has been made to trace the owners of the copyrighted material.

Cover image: jugulator/Shutterstock.com

Library of Congress Cataloging-in-Publication Data

Names: Schmermund, Elizabeth, editor.
Title: Civil disobedience / edited by Elizabeth Schmermund.
Description: New York : Greenhaven Publishing, 2018. | Series: At issue | Includes
  bibliographic references and index. | Audience: Grades 9-12.
Identifiers: LCCN | ISBN 9781534500655 (library bound) | ISBN 9781534500631
  (pbk.)
Subjects: LCSH: Civil disobedience--Juvenile literature. | Nonviolence--Juvenile
  literature. | Social action--Juvenile literature.
Classification: LCC JC328.3 C686 2018 | DDC 303.6?1--dc23

Manfactured in The United States of America

Website: http://greenhavenpublishing.com

Contents

Introduction

F ew would disagree that civil disobedience has been foundational to democratic societies around the world. However, this doesn't mean that people haven't argued against the uses and practicalities of civil disobedience in the past. For example, lawyer and Presidential Medal of Freedom recipient Morris L. Leibman famously declared that civil disobedience was a threat to American society, in an article reprinted many times in the fifty years since it was first published and found in this compendium. Others have argued over the definition of civil disobedience itself, including whether or not the definition allows the use of violence in the pursuit of justice. Yet others have argued over the practicality of such action, particularly if it has the potential of harming a group's interest in the court of public opinion in politically divisive moments such as those we face today.

Very simply, civil disobedience is defined by the New World Encyclopedia as "the active refusal to obey certain laws, demands, and commands of a government or of an occupying power without resorting to physical violence." This definition hinges on the belief that laws themselves can be unjust and that it can be a moral obligation to disobey these unjust laws. Few people would disagree that laws are created by fallible men and women and, thus, can be imperfect and, even more, reflect the prejudices of the time in which they are enacted. For example, slavery and then segregation were legal in the United States from the 1600s, until the Civil Rights Act of 1964 banned all state and local laws that allowed racial segregation to continue. This law, overturning previous laws that had instituted racially discriminatory laws in the first place, was only reversed in light of active non-violent protests and civil disobedience led by such figures as Martin Luther King Jr. In an international context, famous resisters of unjust laws include Nelson Mandela, who fought against apartheid in South Africa, and Mahatma Gandhi, who fought against English rule without representation in India.

Yet another important figure in civil disobedience is Henry David Thoreau, who is often credited with initiating the modern notion of non-violent action. In the mid-nineteenth century, Thoreau refused to pay his taxes in light of his condemnation of certain US policies, including slavery and an escalation of violence in the Mexican-American War. He was jailed for one night before being released when a neighbor paid the taxes that Thoreau owed. However, Thoreau incorporated his experiences and his belief in the duty of citizens to resist their government's unjust laws in the seminal essay "Civil Disobedience" (1849). This work solidified the philosophy behind non-violent resistance to unjust laws and personally influenced famous activists, including King, Mandela, and Gandhi, as well as Rosa Parks, Dolores Huerta, and others.

Since Thoreau, civil disobedience has been perhaps most notably used in the US civil rights movement, where marches, sit-ins, freedom rides, and other forms of protest were used to great effect—and which generated much publicity for activists' causes. But civil disobedience has also been used by war resisters, many of whom have publically refused to pay any taxes when these funds are used by the United States government to fund military actions abroad. The War Resisters League is one of the earliest organizations to create an organized action against US-funded war and was created in 1923 by a New York City teacher named Jessie Wallace Hughan to fight against the drafting of young men into World War I. The War Resisters League is still an active presence today, and its ranks have swelled in the face of many recent and unpopular wars, including the wars in Iraq and Afghanistan during the early twenty-first century. As terrorist threats and wars in the Middle East have proliferated in recent years, members of the War Resisters League have become even more outspoken about their positions and have called on other citizens to resist unjust wars through the best means available—their wallets.

Other fights that non-violent activists have taken on in recent years include protests and mass actions against lax environmental destruction and deregulation, internet freedom, and violence against minorities. A vocal population of environmental activists has leveraged the attention they receive from mass protests to great effect. In particular, non-violent protests against the Dakota Access and Keystone XL pipelines, oil pipelines which activists state would be both detrimental to the environment and to the native populations where these pipes will be laid, have achieved great strides and received media attention in their struggle against corporate interests. Their largely peaceful protests gained particular attention in 2016, when a protest at the Dakota Access pipeline site in North Dakota near the Standing Rock Indian Reservation was broken up by local law enforcement using such methods as tear gas and attack dogs. While incidents such as these drew international criticism and applied political pressure on the US government, these fights continue today.

Another domain in which civil disobedience is playing out today is online, where "hacktivists," as they are known, are undertaking their own versions of "sit-ins" and non-violent disruptions. Internet freedom activists fight against corporate interests online and the censoring of public information through hacking into and otherwise disrupting websites and internet servers. In one notable and tragic case, hacktivist Aaron Swartz, the young cofounder of the website Reddit, committed suicide in 2013 after being charged with sixteen felonies and the possibility of fifty years in prison and millions of dollars in fines. What was his crime? Taking articles from the online academic repository JSTOR and posting them for free in order to protest the pay wall that much important academic information is kept behind. Swartz felt that the internet is a place where information should be shared freely and openly, without needing to pay fees to gain access to knowledge. Unfortunately his act of online civil disobedience cost him his life.

As these new methods and modes of civil disobedience arise, many questions remain unanswered. Is online civil disobedience inherently different than "offline" mass actions? What is the difference between the criminal action of "stealing" and the collection of censored information in the face of unjust laws? Should such activists be punished for their acts of disobedience and is punishment, in fact, integral to civil disobedience itself? How do acts of civil disobedience sway public opinion in the partisan world of politics? And, while civil disobedience has historically been used in the pursuit of more liberal political goals, can it also be used for conservative interests, such as pro-life movements, as well?

As the United States—and indeed, the world—appears to be more divided over political issues now than in past years, the role of civil disobedience will increase as grassroots activists take a stand against what they perceive as unjust laws advocated for by big corporations and instituted by corrupt politicians. How will this play out? We can't know that yet. But this text will help you to understand the history of civil disobedience and its risks—as well as to suggest possible ways non-violent action will be used to great effect in the future.

1

Civil Disobedience Has Successfully Been Used Many Times in the Past

New World Encyclopedia Editors

The New World Encyclopedia is an online collection of articles on a variety of topics written by certified experts.

In this encyclopedia entry, the definition of civil disobedience is supplied along with important instances of its use. It is important to note that, while this viewpoint does not offer a resolute "side" per se, it does affirm the importance of civil disobedience when placed in historical context. Indeed, civil disobedience has been used many times in the past and appears to be an integral part of many democratic governments. Thus, it would bear out that civil disobedience would continue to play an important and expected role in modern societies today.

Civil disobedience encompasses the active refusal to obey certain laws, demands, and commands of a government or of an occupying power without resorting to physical violence. Based on the position that laws can be unjust, and that there are human rights that supersede such laws, civil disobedience developed in an effort to achieve social change when all channels of negotiation failed. The act of civil disobedience involves the breaking of a law, and as such is a crime and the participants expect and are willing to suffer punishment in order to make their case known.

"Civil Disobedience," New World Encyclopedia. https://www.newworldencyclopedia.org/entry/Civil_disobedience. Licensed under CC BY-SA 3.0.

Civil disobedience has been used successfully in nonviolent resistance movements in India (Mahatma Gandhi's social welfare campaigns and campaigns to speed up independence from the British Empire), in South Africa in the fight against apartheid, and in the American Civil Rights Movement, among others. Until all people live under conditions in which their human rights are fully met, and there is prosperity and happiness for all, civil disobedience may be necessary to accomplish those goals.

Definition

The American author Henry David Thoreau pioneered the modern theory behind the practice of civil disobedience in his 1849 essay, Civil Disobedience, originally titled Resistance to Civil Government. The driving idea behind the essay was that of self-reliance, and how one is in morally good standing as long as one can "get off another man's back;" so one doesn't have to physically fight the government, but one must not support it or have it support one (if one is against it). This essay has had a wide influence on many later practitioners of civil disobedience. Thoreau explained his reasons for having refused to pay taxes as an act of protest against slavery and against the Mexican-American War.

Civil disobedience can be distinguished from other active forms of protest, such as rioting, because of its passivity and non-violence.

Theories and techniques

In seeking an active form of civil disobedience, one may choose to deliberately break certain laws, such as by forming a peaceful blockade or occupying a facility illegally. Protesters practice this non-violent form of civil disorder with the expectation that they will be arrested, or even attacked or beaten by the authorities. Protesters often undergo training in advance on how to react to arrest or to attack, so that they will do so in a manner that quietly or limply resists without threatening the authorities.

For example, Mahatma Gandhi outlined the following rules:

1. A civil resister (or satyagrahi) will harbor no anger

2. He will suffer the anger of the opponent

3. In so doing he will put up with assaults from the opponent, never retaliate; but he will not submit, out of fear of punishment or the like, to any order given in anger

4. When any person in authority seeks to arrest a civil resister, he will voluntarily submit to the arrest, and he will not resist the attachment or removal of his own property, if any, when it is sought to be confiscated by authorities

5. If a civil resister has any property in his possession as a trustee, he will refuse to surrender it, even though in defending it he might lose his life. He will, however, never retaliate

6. Retaliation includes swearing and cursing

7. Therefore a civil resister will never insult his opponent, and therefore also not take part in many of the newly coined cries which are contrary to the spirit of ahimsa

8. A civil resister will not salute the Union Jack, nor will he insult it or officials, English or Indian

9. In the course of the struggle if anyone insults an official or commits an assault upon him, a civil resister will protect such official or officials from the insult or attack even at the risk of his life

Gandhi distinguished between his idea of satyagraha and the passive resistance of the west. Gandhi's rules were specific to the Indian independence movement, but many of the ideas are used by those practicing civil disobedience around the world. The most general principle on which civil disobedience rests is non-violence and passivity, as protesters refuse to retaliate or take action.

The writings of Leo Tolstoy were influential on Gandhi. Aside from his literature, Tolstoy was famous for advocating pacifism as a method of social reform. Tolstoy himself was influenced by the Sermon on the Mount, in which Jesus tells his followers to turn the other cheek when attacked. Tolstoy's philosophy is outlined in his work, Kingdom of God is Within You.

Many who practice civil disobedience do so out of religious faith, and clergy often participate in or lead actions of civil disobedience. A notable example is Philip Berrigan, a Roman Catholic priest who was arrested dozens of times in acts of civil disobedience in antiwar protests.

Philosophy of civil disobedience

The practice of civil disobedience comes into conflict with the laws of the country in which it takes place. Advocates of civil disobedience must strike a balance between obeying these laws and fighting for their beliefs without creating a society of anarchy. Immanuel Kant developed the "categorical imperative" in which every person's action should be just so that it could be taken to be a universal law. In civil disobedience, if every person were to act that way, there is the danger that anarchy would result.

Therefore, those practicing civil disobedience do so when no other recourse is available, often regarding the law to be broken as contravening a higher principle, one that falls within the categorical imperative. Knowing that breaking the law is a criminal act, and therefore that punishment will ensue, civil disobedience marks the law as unjust and the lawbreaker as willing to suffer in order that justice may ensue for others.

Within the framework of democracy, ideally rule by the people, debate exists over whether or not practices such as civil disobedience are in fact not illegal because they are legitimate expressions of the people's discontent. When the incumbent government breaks the existing social contract, some would argue that citizens are fully justified in rebelling against it as the government is not fulfilling the citizens' needs. Thus, one might consider civil disobedience validated when legislation enacted by the government is in violation of natural law.[1]

The principle of civil disobedience is recognized as justified, even required, under exceptional circumstance such as war crimes. In the Nuremberg Trials following World War II, individuals were held accountable for their failure to resist laws that caused extreme suffering to innocent people.

Examples of civil disobedience

Civil disobedience was used to great effect in India by Gandhi, in Poland by the Solidarity movement against Communism, in South Africa against apartheid, and in the United States by Martin Luther King, Jr. against racism. It was also used as a major tactic of nationalist movements in former colonies in Africa and Asia prior to their gaining independence.

India

Gandhi first used his ideas of satyagraha in India on a local level in 1918, in Champaran, a district in the state of Bihar, and in Kheda in the state of Gujarat. In response to poverty, scant resources, the social evils of alcoholism and untouchability, and overall British indifference and hegemony, Gandhi proposed satyagraha—non-violent, mass civil disobedience. While it was strictly non-violent, Gandhi was proposing real action, a real revolt that the oppressed peoples of India were dying to undertake.

Gandhi insisted that the protesters neither allude to or try to propagate the concept of Swaraj, or Independence. The action was not about political freedom, but a revolt against abject tyranny amidst a terrible humanitarian disaster. While accepting participants and help from other parts of India, Gandhi insisted that no other district or province revolt against the government, and that the Indian National Congress not get involved apart from issuing resolutions of support, to prevent the British from giving it cause to use extensive suppressive measures and brand the revolts as treason.

In both states, Gandhi organized civil resistance on the part of tens of thousands of landless farmers and poor farmers with small lands, who were forced to grow indigo and other cash crops instead of the food crops necessary for their survival. It was an area of extreme poverty, unhygienic villages, rampant alcoholism and untouchables. In addition to the crop-growing restrictions, the British had levied an oppressive tax. Gandhi's solution was to establish an ashram near Kheda, where scores of supporters and volunteers from the region did a detailed study of the villages—itemizing atrocities, suffering, and degenerate living conditions. He led the villagers in a clean up movement, encouraging social reform, and building schools and hospitals.

For his efforts, Gandhi was arrested by police on the charges of unrest and was ordered to leave Bihar. Hundreds of thousands of people protested and rallied outside the jail, police stations, and courts demanding his release, which was unwillingly granted. Gandhi then organized protests and strikes against the landlords, who finally agreed to more pay and allowed the farmers to determine what crops to raise. The government canceled tax collections until the famine ended.

In Kheda, Gandhi's associate, Sardar Vallabhai Patel led the actions, guided by Gandhi's ideas. The revolt was astounding in terms of discipline and unity. Even when all their personal property, land, and livelihood were seized, a vast majority of Kheda's farmers remained firmly united in support of Patel. Gujaratis sympathetic to the revolt in other parts resisted the government machinery, and helped to shelter the relatives and property of the protesting peasants. Those Indians who sought to buy the confiscated lands were ostracized from society. Although nationalists like Sardul Singh Caveeshar called for sympathetic revolts in other parts, Gandhi and Patel firmly rejected the idea.

The government finally sought to foster an honorable agreement for both parties. The tax for the year in question and the next would be suspended, and the increase in rate reduced, while all confiscated property would be returned. The success in these situations spread throughout the country.

Gandhi used Satyagraha on a national level in 1919, the year the Rowlatt Act was passed, allowing the government to imprison persons accused of sedition without trial. Also that year, in Punjab, 1-2,000 people were wounded and 400 or more were killed by

British troops in the Amritsar massacre.[2] A traumatized and angry nation engaged in retaliatory acts of violence against the British. Gandhi criticized both the British and the Indians. Arguing that all violence was evil and could not be justified, he convinced the national party to pass a resolution offering condolences to British victims and condemning the Indian riots.[3] At the same time, these incidents led Gandhi to focus on complete self-government and complete control of all government institutions. This matured into Swaraj, or complete individual, spiritual, political independence.

The first move in the Swaraj non-violent campaign was the famous Salt March. The government monopolized the salt trade, making it illegal for anyone else to produce it, even though it was readily available to those near the sea coast. Because the tax on salt affected everyone, it was a good focal point for protest. Gandhi marched 400 kilometers (248 miles) from Ahmedabad to Dandi, Gujarat, to make his own salt near the sea. In the 23 days (March 12 to April 6) it took, the march gathered thousands. Once in Dandi, Gandhi encouraged everyone to make and trade salt. In the next days and weeks, thousands made or bought illegal salt, and by the end of the month, more than 60,000 had been arrested. It was one of his most successful campaigns. Although Gandhi himself strictly adhered to non-violence throughout his life, even fasting until violence ceased, his dream of a unified, independent India was not achieved and his own life was taken by an assassin. Nevertheless, his ideals have lived on, inspiring those in many other countries to use non-violent civil disobedience against oppressive and unjust governments.

Poland

Civil disobedience was a tactic used by the Polish in protest of the former communist government. In the 1970s and 1980s, there occurred a deepening crisis within Soviet-style societies brought about by declining morale, worsening economic conditions (a shortage economy), and the growing stresses of the Cold War.[4] After a brief period of economic boom, from 1975, the policies of the

Polish government, led by Party First Secretary Edward Gierek, precipitated a slide into increasing depression, as foreign debt mounted.[5] In June 1976, the first workers' strikes took place, involving violent incidents at factories in Radom and Ursus.[6]

On October 16, 1978, the Bishop of Kraków, Karol Wojtyła, was elected Pope John Paul II. A year later, during his first pilgrimage to Poland, his masses were attended by millions of his countrymen. The Pope called for the respecting of national and religious traditions and advocated for freedom and human rights, while denouncing violence. To many Poles, he represented a spiritual and moral force that could be set against brute material forces; he was a bellwether of change, and became an important symbol—and supporter—of changes to come. He was later to define the concept of "solidarity" in his Encyclical Sollicitudo Rei Socialis (December 30, 1987).[7]

On July of 1980, the government of Edward Gierek, facing an economic crisis, decided to raise the prices while slowing the growth of the wages. A wave of strikes and factory occupations began at once.[4] At the Lenin Shipyard in Gdańsk, workers were outraged at the sacking of Anna Walentynowicz, a popular crane operator and well-known activist who became a spark that pushed them into action.[8] The workers were led by electrician Lech Wałęsa, a former shipyard worker who had been dismissed in 1976, and who arrived at the shipyard on August 14.[4] The strike committee demanded rehiring of Anna Walentynowicz and Lech Wałęsa, raising a monument to the casualties of 1970, respecting of worker's rights and additional social demands.

By August 21, most of Poland was affected by the strikes, from coastal shipyards to the mines of the Upper Silesian Industrial Area. Thanks to popular support within Poland, as well as to international support and media coverage, the Gdańsk workers held out until the government gave in to their demands. Though concerned with labor union matters, the Gdańsk agreement enabled citizens to introduce democratic changes within the communist political structure and was regarded as a first step toward dismantling the Party's monopoly of power.[9]

Buoyed by the success of the strike, on September 17, the representatives of Polish workers, including Lech Wałęsa, formed a nationwide trade union, Solidarity (Niezależny Samorządny Związek Zawodowy "Solidarność"). On December 16, 1980, the Monument to fallen Shipyard Workers was unveiled. On January 15, 1981, a delegation from Solidarity, including Lech Wałęsa, met Pope John Paul II in Rome. Between September 5 and 10 and September 26 to October 7, the first national congress of Solidarity was held, and Lech Wałęsa was elected its president.

In the meantime Solidarity transformed from a trade union into a social movement. Over the next 500 days following the Gdańsk Agreement, 9 to 10 million workers, intellectuals, and students joined it or its sub-organizations. It was the first and only recorded time in the history that a quarter of a country's population have voluntarily joined a single organization. "History has taught us that there is no bread without freedom," the Solidarity program stated a year later. "What we had in mind were not only bread, butter, and sausage but also justice, democracy, truth, legality, human dignity, freedom of convictions, and the repair of the republic."

Using strikes and other protest actions, Solidarity sought to force a change in the governmental policies. At the same time it was careful to never use force or violence, to avoid giving the government any excuse to bring the security forces into play. Solidarity's influence led to the intensification and spread of anti-communist ideals and movements throughout the countries of the Eastern Bloc, weakening their communist governments.

In 1983, Lech Wałęsa received the Nobel Prize for Peace, but the Polish government refused to issue him a passport and allow him to leave the country. Finally, Roundtable Talks between the weakened Polish government and Solidarity-led opposition led to semi-free elections in 1989. By the end of August, a Solidarity-led coalition government was formed, and in December, Lech Wałęsa was elected president.

South Africa

Both Archbishop Desmond Tutu and Steve Biko advocated civil disobedience in the fight against apartheid. The result can be seen in such notable events as the 1989 Purple Rain Protest, and the Cape Town Peace March, which defied apartheid laws.

Purple rain protest

On September 2, 1989, four days before South Africa's racially segregated parliament held its elections, a police water cannon with purple dye was turned on thousands of Mass Democratic Movement supporters who poured into the city in an attempt to march on South Africa's Parliament on Burg Street in Cape Town.[10] Protesters were warned to disperse but instead knelt in the street and the water cannon was turned on them. Some remained kneeling while others fled. Some had their feet knocked out from under them by the force of the jet. A group of about 50 protesters streaming with purple dye, ran from Burg Street, down to the parade. They were followed by another group of clergymen and others who were stopped in Plein Street. Some were then arrested. On the Parade, a large contingent of police arrested everyone they could find who had purple dye on them. When they were booed by the crowd, police dispersed them. About 250 people marching under a banner stating, "The People Shall Govern," dispersed at the intersection of Darling Street and Sir Lowry Road after being stopped by police.[11]

Cape Town peace march

On September 12, 1989, 30,000 Capetonians marched in support of peace and the end of apartheid. The event lead by Mayor Gordon Oliver, Archbishop Tutu, Rev Frank Chikane, Moulana Faried Esack, and other religious leaders was held in defiance of the government's ban on political marches. The demonstration forced President de Klerk to relinquish the hardline against transformation, and the eventual unbanning of the ANC, and other political parties, and the release of Nelson Mandela less than six months later.

The United States

There is a long history of civil disobedience in the United States. One of the first practitioners was Henry David Thoreau whose 1849 essay, Civil Disobedience, is considered a defining exposition of the modern form of this type of action. It advocates the idea that people should not support any government attempting unjust actions. Thoreau was motivated by his opposition to the institution of slavery and the fighting of the Mexican-American War. Those participating in the movement for women's suffrage also engaged in civil disobedience.[12] The labor movement in the early twentieth century used sit-in strikes at plants and other forms of civil disobedience. Civil disobedience has also been used by those wishing to protest the Vietnam War, apartheid in South Africa, and against American intervention in Central America.[13]

King is perhaps most famous for his "I Have a Dream" speech, given in front of the Lincoln Memorial during the 1963 March on Washington for Jobs and Freedom.

Martin Luther King, Jr. is one of the most famous activists who used civil disobedience to achieve reform. In 1953, at the age of twenty-four, King became pastor of the Dexter Avenue Baptist Church, in Montgomery, Alabama. King correctly recognized that organized, nonviolent protest against the racist system of southern segregation known as Jim Crow laws would lead to extensive media coverage of the struggle for black equality and voting rights. Indeed, journalistic accounts and televised footage of the daily deprivation and indignities suffered by southern blacks, and of segregationist violence and harassment of civil rights workers and marchers, produced a wave of sympathetic public opinion that made the Civil Rights Movement the single most important issue in American politics in the early-1960s. King organized and led marches for blacks' right to vote, desegregation, labor rights, and other basic civil rights. Most of these rights were successfully enacted into United States law with the passage of the Civil Rights Act of 1964 and the Voting Rights Act of 1965.

On December 1, 1955, Rosa Parks was arrested for refusing to comply with the Jim Crow law that required her to give up her seat to a white man. The Montgomery Bus Boycott, led by King, soon followed. The boycott lasted for 382 days, the situation becoming so tense that King's house was bombed. King was arrested during this campaign, which ended with a United States Supreme Court decision outlawing racial segregation on all public transport.

King was instrumental in the founding of the Southern Christian Leadership Conference (SCLC) in 1957, a group created to harness the moral authority and organizing power of black churches to conduct nonviolent protests in the service of civil rights reform. King continued to dominate the organization. King was an adherent of the philosophies of nonviolent civil disobedience used successfully in India by Mahatma Gandhi, and he applied this philosophy to the protests organized by the SCLC.

Civil disobedience has continued to be used into the twenty-first century in the United States by protesters against numerous alleged injustices, including discrimination against homosexuals by church and other authorities, American intervention in Iraq, as well as by anti-abortion protesters and others.

Notes

1. Peter Suber, Civil Disobedience, Earlham College. Retrieved May 5, 2007.
2. www.mkgandhi.org, Biography. Retrieved June 12, 2008.
3. R. Gandhi, Patel: A Life, p. 82.
4. 4.0 4.1 4.2 Colin Baker, The rise of Solidarnosc, International Socialism.]] Retrieved July 10, 2006.
5. Keith John Lepak, Prelude to Solidarity (Columbia University Press, 1989, ISBN 0-231-06608-2).
6. Barbara J. Falk, The Dilemmas of Dissidence in East-Central Europe: Citizen Intellectuals and Philosopher Kings (Central European University Press, 2003, ISBN 963-9241-39-3).
7. George Weigel, The Final Revolution: The Resistance Church and the Collapse of Communism (Oxford University Press, 2003, ISBN 0-19-516664-7), p. 136.
8. BBC News, The birth of Solidarity. Retrieved July 10, 2006.
9. Norman Davies, God's Playground (2005, ISBN 0-231-12819-3).

10. Weekend Argus, "Purple Rain halts city demo," front page, Saturday, September 2, 1989.

11. Weekend Argus, "Purple Rain halts city demo," front page, Saturday, September 2, 1989.

12. The National Archives, Teaching With Documents: Woman Suffrage and the 19th Amendment. Retrieved April 30, 2007.

13. AIDS Coalition to Unleash Power, History of Mass Nonviolent Action. Retrieved April 30, 2007.

References

Arendt, Hannah. 1972. *Crises of the Republic: Lying in Politics; Civil Disobedience; On Violence; Thoughts on Politics and Revolution*. Harvest Books. ISBN 0156232006.

Hendrick, George. 2005. W*hy Not Every Man? African Americans and Civil Disobedience in the Quest for the Dream*. Ivan R. Dee, Publisher. ISBN 1566636450.

Polner, Murray, and Jim O'Grady. 2001. *Disarmed and Dangerous: The Radical Life and Times of Daniel and Philip Berrigan, Brothers in Religious Faith and Civil Disobedience*. Westview Press. ISBN 0813334497.

Thoreau, Henry David. 2005. *Civil Disobedience And Other Essays: the Collected Essays of Henry David Thoreau*. Digireads.com ISBN 978-1420925227.

Thoreau, Henry David. [1848] 2007. *On the Duty of Civil Disobedience*. Book Jungle. ISBN 978-1594625268.

Tolstoy, Leo. 1987. *Writings on Civil Disobedience and Nonviolence*. New Society Pub. ISBN 0865711097.

Zinn, Howard. 1997. *The Zinn Reader: Writings on Disobedience and Democracy*. Seven Stories Press. ISBN 1888363541.

2

Philosophers and Activists Have Long Debated the Use and Morality of Civil Disobedience

Donald M. Borchert

Donald M. Borchert is an author and academic who has edited many important anthologies in philosophy, including The Encyclopedia of Philosophy.

This viewpoint, taken from The Encyclopedia of Philosophy, *an important compendium of philosophical thought, examines how philosophers and activists such as Martin Luther King Jr. interpreted both the definition of civil disobedience and its morality. These philosophical interpretations are not black and white and, as such, the conclusion drawn falls into a gray area. Thus, the viewpoint ends with the perhaps unsatisfying but accurate view that civil disobedience can be morally just in some circumstances, while not in others. Indeed, as the article states, "People who agree that civil disobedience can be justified in theory can still disagree about whether it is justified in practice."*

The idea of civil disobedience comes out of the tradition of social and political protest whose best known advocates are the 19th century American transcendentalist Henry David Thoreau, the Indian reformer Mohandas Gandhi, and the American civil rights leader, Martin Luther King, Jr. While the idea of civil disobedience

"Civil Disobedience," in D. Borchert, ed., *The Encyclopedia of Philosophy*, 2nd ed., Macmillan Reference, 2006, Reprinted by permission.

has diverse roots, the views of these activist/thinkers set the stage for academic and popular discussion.

Philosophical discussions of civil disobedience generally focus on two questions. First, what is civil disobedience? Second, can acts of civil disobedience be morally justified?

Defining "civil disobedience"

The definition of civil disobedience that best accords with the tradition of Thoreau, Gandhi, and King categorizes acts as civil disobedience if they have four features. They must be: 1) illegal, 2) nonviolent, 3) public, and 4) done to protest a governmental law or policy.

Thoreau's refusal to pay his taxes has all these features. It was illegal, nonviolent, and was public. (Unlike a tax evader, Thoreau did not hide his not paying.) And, it was done to protest policies of the United States government that Thoreau thought were seriously unjust—support of slavery and an aggressive war against Mexico.

Actions like Thoreau's are sometimes described as "conscientious refusal," refusing to obey a law that requires one to act immorally. Some people see conscientious refusal as different from publicly protesting a policy, but the two usually go together. Generally, people who refuse to obey unjust laws hope that their act will stimulate others to see that the law is wrong and to work for change. Thoreau spoke publicly about the reasons for his act, and his lecture became the classic essay "Civil Disobedience."

Gandhi and King went beyond individual conscientious refusal and organized large numbers of people to disobey the law as a means of protest. These illegal acts were intended to publicize serious injustices and to rally support for change. If enough people were to disobey an unjust law, it might be impossible for a government to enforce it.

Acts of civil disobedience cover a spectrum, ranging from a) conscientious refusal by individuals to b) symbolic disobedience that is meant to convey a message about the wrongness of government policy to c) large scale acts of disobedience that aim to render a government unable to carry out its policies.

Not everyone would accept the definition given above. Some argue that civil disobedients must accept the punishment, but this does not seem necessary. For example, someone who publicly burns a draft card might flee the country if the punishment were extremely severe; yet the original act would still be civil disobedience, even if the act of fleeing is not. John Rawls has argued that civil disobedience addresses a community's sense of justice, but this overlooks the fact that a community can have mistaken or conflicting conceptions of justice. Finally, some argue that civil disobedience can be violent, but this overlooks the connotations of the word "civil" and violates the tradition of Gandhi and King, who were explicitly committed to nonviolent strategies of resistance. Moreover, since violent acts require stronger types of justification, including them in the definition complicates the evaluation of civil disobedience. Violent acts will have to be distinguished from nonviolent ones when we try to see if civil disobedience can be morally justified. In the end, the test of definitions is that they help to clarify matters, and lumping together violent and nonviolent acts in this case does not seem helpful.

Using the definition above, the question "Is civil disobedience ever morally justified?" can be understood to mean "Is it ever morally permissible to engage in nonviolent, public violations of the law in order to protest a governmental law or policy?"

The duty to obey the law

Asking whether civil disobedience can be morally justified presupposes that there is some moral duty to obey the law. If there were no such moral duty, then breaking the law would not need a special justification. In addition, people who think that civil disobedience can never be justified must believe that the moral duty to obey the law is absolute and can never be over-ridden by other moral concerns.

Socrates' arguments in the *Crito* are often taken as a source of the view that people must always obey the law. Socrates appears to argue that people must always obey the law because the state is like a parent and one must obey one's parents, that the state has benefited him and therefore should be obeyed, and that he has made a tacit agreement to obey the laws by living in Athens all his life. In the *Apology*, however, Socrates states that he will disobey the law if it requires him to violate the commands of the gods. Socrates, then, is a source of both the individualist tradition that approves civil disobedience and the authoritarian, statist tradition that condemns it.

In his *Leviathan*, Thomas Hobbes provides a famous argument for the duty of obedience to law. He argued that recognition of government's authority is justified because it is the only way for people to avoid a state of nature in which everyone is a threat to everyone else. If everyone followed their own judgment and recognized no legal authority, this would lead to a situation of unlimited conflict in which life is "nasty, brutish, and short." Hobbes thought that peace could be achieved if people agree to obey a sovereign who enforces the laws. If everyone claims a right to act according to their own judgment and to disregard the law, then government would be undermined, and there would be a return to anarchy and a "war of all against all." In short, individuals must trade away their personal autonomy if peace and security are to be possible.

In a much discussed argument from the 1960s, Robert Paul Wolff turned Hobbes' argument on its head in order to defend a version of philosophical anarchism. Wolff agrees with Hobbes that governments claim authority over what citizens should do and thus take away personal autonomy. But, Wolff claimed, personal autonomy—deciding what is right and wrong for oneself and acting on those decisions—can never legitimately be traded away. Therefore, governmental authority can never be morally legitimate. From Wolff's anarchist perspective, it is obedience to law rather than disobedience that is morally questionable.

There is also a cynical tradition that sees laws as devices for protecting the interests of the rich and powerful. Thrasymachus, a character in Plato's *Republic*, defined justice as whatever is in the interests of the stronger. This idea is echoed in the Marxist view that the legal system is a prop for the protecting the property and power of the wealthy. This cynical perspective suggests that it is foolish to believe in a moral obligation to obey the law.

Justifying civil disobedience

Debates about civil disobedience are often conducted in all or nothing terms. They presuppose either a) that there is an absolute obligation to obey the law no matter what, or b) that there is no obligation to obey the law at all. From this perspective, support for civil disobedience leads to anarchism while opposition to it requires mindless conformity to law.

A different tradition emerges from John Locke's *Second Treatise on Civil Government*. While Locke argued that governments and laws could be legitimate and should be taken seriously, he also defended a right of revolution in cases where the government violates the rights that it is supposed to defend. According to Locke, the duty to obey is conditional on the nature of the government. There is no duty to obey a tyrannical government. This Lockean view acknowledges a general moral duty to obey the law while recognizing that there are circumstances in which disobedience—and even revolution—might be justified. Locke's view is echoed in the American *Declaration of Independence* which affirms a right to "alter or abolish" a government that violates its people's rights.

Defenders of civil disobedience, then, need not be anarchists. They can recognize the moral force of the law while at the same time believing that the moral force of the law is conditional. When the right conditions do not exist, various forms of disobedience, including civil disobedience, may be justified. If the conditions that warrant obedience do exist, then people who violate the law are acting wrongly. Because obedience to law can be morally required in some cases and not in others, civil disobedience can be justified in some cases and not in others.

The argument for civil disobedience is strongest when a specific law requires people to act immorally. A broader justification for disobedience arises when a government lacks legitimacy. Gandhi's campaign for Indian independence, for example, challenged the legitimacy of British colonial rule. If British rule was illegitimate, then there was no moral duty to obey British laws. Still, for both moral and tactical reasons, Gandhi used civil disobedience very selectively.

King's defense of selective obedience

While there are plausible justifications for disobedience to some laws and some governments, a serious problem faces people who engage in civil disobedience but nonetheless appeal to others to obey the law. Martin Luther King Jr's classic "Letter from Birmingham Jail" discusses just this problem. Critics charged that King was inconsistent because he urged segregationists to obey laws that prohibited racial discrimination at the same time that King and his followers stated their willingness to violate other laws. If selective obedience was permissible for King, why was it not permissible for his opponents?

King defended himself by providing criteria for justified disobedience. He argued that it is morally permissible to disobey the law a) when the law itself is unjust because it "degrades human personality" rather than respecting people, b) when the laws are binding on a minority group but do not bind the majority that imposes it, c) when those who are mistreated are deprived of rights of democratic participation in the process of enacting the law, or d) when a proper law is unjustly applied so as to deprive people of their rights of protest. These conditions, he argued, were met by those campaigning for racial equality but not by those who supported segregation.

King's argument shows how one can consistently defend the right to disobey the law and also take obedience to law seriously. He recognizes a strong presumption in favor of obedience but argues that the presumption is over-ridden in the kinds of circumstances he describes.

Unjustified civil disobedience

Acts of civil disobedience are not as difficult to justify as forms of protest that use violence. Nonetheless, acts of civil disobedience can be morally wrong. For example, they can be committed on behalf of an unjust cause. Thoreau, Gandhi, and King all protested serious evils, but if a person mistakenly believes that a law or policy is unjust, then an act of disobedience against it will not be morally justified. Moreover, even if a law or policy is bad, its defects may not be serious enough to justify violating the law. If obedience to law is something we expect of others when they disagree with a law, then we are not justified if we disobey laws simply because we disagree with them. Disobedience must be reserved for very serious cases, and even then, it may not be justified if legal means are available for effectively promoting change. It is only when effective, legal means are unavailable that civil disobedience is permissible. Finally, such acts can be wrong if they undermine just and valuable institutions.

A strong case, then, can be made for the view that civil disobedience can be morally justified under certain conditions. Whether specific acts of civil disobedience are justified, however, is often controversial. This is because people often disagree about the seriousness of the evils being opposed, the availability of other effective means of protest, and the long term effects on valuable institutions and practices. People who agree that civil disobedience can be justified in theory can still disagree about whether it is justified in practice.

Bibliography

Bedau, Hugo Adam, ed. *Civil Disobedience in Focus.* London: Routledge, 1991.

Gandhi, M. K. *Non-violent Resistance.* New York: Schocken Books, 1961.

Hobbes, Thomas. *Leviathan.* Many editions.

King, Martin Luther, Jr. "Letter from a Birmingham Jail." In *Why We Can't Wait.* New York: Signet Books, 1964.

Locke, John. *Second Treatise on Civil Government.* Many editions.

Nathanson, Stephen. *Should We Consent to Be Governed?*, 2nd ed. Belmont, CA: Wadsworth, 2001.

Plato. *Apology, Crito, Republic.* Many editions.

Rawls, John. "The Justification of Civil Disobedience." In *John Rawls: Collected Papers*, ed. Samuel Freedman. Cambridge, MA: Harvard University Press, 1999.

Thoreau, Henry David. "Civil Disobedience" and "A Plea for Captain John Brown." In *Walden and Other Writings of Henry David Thoreau*, ed. Brooks Atkinson. New York: Modern Library, 1950.

Wolff, Robert Paul. *In Defense of Anarchism,* 2nd ed. New York: Harper and Row, 1976.

Zinn, Howard. *Disobedience and Democracy: Nine Fallacies on Law and Order.* New York: Vintage Books, 1968.

3

Civil Disobedience Is a Threat to Our Society

Morris L. Leibman

Leibman was a senior partner at the Chicago law firm of Sidley & Austin and the founder of the National Strategy Forum, a nonprofit dedicated to research and discussion in foreign affairs. He was awarded the Presidential Medal of Freedom in 1981 and passed away in 1992.

In this viewpoint, Morris L. Leibman argues that Americans are living in one of the freest societies ever. It is important to note, however, when his argument is being made. Leibman first delivered the following text as a speech at the American Bar Association Meeting in 1964. This was during the height of the civil rights movement, when African Americans and their supporters used civil disobedience to protest against unjust laws that instituted segregation. It is important to judge Leibman's argument, particularly that the "jungle lawlessness of the frontier demonstrated to the pioneers that law was essential to the establishment of civilization," in light of this historical context.

Morris I. Leibman (1911–1992) was a partner in the law firm Sidley and Austin. He was awarded the Presidential Medal of Freedom in 1981 by President Ronald Reagan.

This article, which originally appeared in the Freeman *in December 1964, is an adaptation of Mr. Leibman's address before the American Bar Association Meeting, Criminal Law Section, in*

"Civil Disobedience: A Threat to Our Society Under Law," by Morris I. Leibman, Foundation for Economic Education, July 1, 1992. https://fee.org/articles/civil-disobedience-a-threat-to-our-society-under-law/. Licensed under CC BY 4.0 International.

the summer of that year. As we again face challenges to our society and its rule of law, his ideas merit a careful re-examination.

Woodrow Wilson once said: "A nation which does not remember what it was yesterday, does not know what it is today, nor what it is trying to do. We are trying to do a futile thing if we do not know where we came from or what we have been about."

In seeking to improve tomorrow, it is our duty to remember where we have been and reflect on where we are.

We live in that instant of time when it can be said that never before have the people in this country enjoyed so many material goods, however "imperfect" their distribution. Never before have we had as much mechanical, electronic, and scientific equipment with which to subdue the natural obstacles of the universe. But the multiplication of consumer wealth is subordinate to our greatest accomplishment—the fashioning of the law society [one that operates under the rule of law].

Never in the history of mankind have so many lived so freely, so rightfully, so humanely. This open democratic republic is man's highest achievement—not only for what it has already accomplished, but more importantly because it affords the greatest opportunity for orderly change and the realization of man's self-renewing aspirations. Our goals, as set forth in the Declaration, have been buttressed by a Constitution, a system of checks and balances, a mechanism judicial, legislative, and executive which permits the continuation of Western civilization's spirited dialogue. This unhampered dialogue makes possible the opportunity to continuously approximate, through our legislative and judicial system, our moral and spiritual goals.

The long history of man is one of pain and suffering, blood and tears, to create these parameters for progress. This noble and unique experiment of ours over a hundred years ago, lived through the cruelty of a massive civil war to test whether such a unique system could endure. It did. It has. It will. Let us always remember that the law society is the pinnacle of man's struggle to date—the foundation for his future hope.

There is an obligation to that law society. It was stated by Abraham Lincoln in these passionate words: "Let every American, every lover of liberty, every well-wisher to his posterity swear by the blood of the Revolution never to violate in the least particular the laws of the country . . . . Let every man remember that to violate the law is to trample on the blood of his father, and to tear the charter of his own and his children's liberty. Let reverence for the laws be breathed by every American mother to the lisping babe that prattles on her lap; let it be taught in schools, in seminaries, and in colleges; let it be written in primers, spelling books, and in almanacs; let it be preached from the pulpit, proclaimed in legislative halls and enforced in courts of justice. And in short, let it become the political religion of the nation; and let the old and the young, the rich and the poor, the grave and the gay of all sexes and tongues and colors and conditions, sacrifice unceasingly upon its altars."

No society whether free or tyrannical can give its citizens the "right" to break the law. There can be no law to which obedience is optional, no command to which the state attaches an "if you please."

What has happened to us? Why is it necessary, at this moment, in this forum to repeat what should be axiomatic and accepted? Many, many words more eloquent than mine have examined from every angle the genesis, the roots, the grievances, the despair, the bitterness, the emotion, the frustration that have resulted in the tragedies of these days.

Responsible Citizenship

Now what is the responsibility of a citizen—the majestic title bestowed on those of us who create and share in the values of the law society? Let there be no question of where we stand on human rights and our rejection of discrimination. Surely the continuing social task for the morally sensitive citizen is to impart reality to the yet unachieved ideal of full and equal participation by all and in all our values and opportunities.

Let's not forget there is nothing new in violence. Violence has throughout mankind's history been too often a way of life. Whole continents have been involved in riot, rebellion, and revolution. Human rights problems exist in India, in Asia, in the Middle East, and in Africa. We cannot sanction terror in our cities. Retaliation is not justified by bitterness or past disillusionment. No individual or group at any time, for any reason, has a right to exact self-determined retribution. All too often, retaliation injures the innocent at random and provokes counter-retaliation against those equally innocent.

Our imperfections do not justify tearing down the structures which have given us our progress. The only solution is the free and open law society. In times when man's progress seems painfully slow on any one issue, we might also consider how well we are doing on all issues compared to most areas of the world over most of the world's history.

In this frame of reference let us identify certain current forces whose aim is to destroy the law society.

Ethnological warfare, the inciting of dissension and conflicts between nationalities and races, has been a widely exploited revolutionary tactic. Communists were long instructed to change passive attitudes to "activist" attitudes, to intensify the struggle at all levels at all times. Communists have had their imitators, who mimic, under many "theories" and many labels, doctrines which reject law and order. The Nazis, the Malcolm X's, the Ku Klux Klanners have repeatedly and directly challenged our principles and insisted on taking "law" in their own hands.

The jungle lawlessness of the frontier demonstrated to the pioneers that law was essential to the establishment of civilization. It was not the destruction of the buffalo, or the rise of fences, or fast-draw gunmen that tamed the wilderness. It was the installation of American juridical proceedings that enabled our people to weld together the disparate territories destined to become an organic nation.

Semantic Traps

I am also deeply troubled by certain concepts which have sought acceptability: the idea of "Freedom *Now*" and the idea of "Righteous Civil Disobedience." In my opinion both terms are semantic traps and only add heat to the problems of freedom and justice for all. It is a further semantic trap to divide the discourse on civil disobedience into a stereotype of liberalism vs. conservatism.

"Freedom Now" is an illusion. The desire for self-expression can be satisfied only in an atmosphere of freedom, and freedom is not absolute. It exists only within the necessary restraining measures of society.

I wish it were possible to have heaven on earth. I wish it were possible to have the ideals of justice and freedom in all their perfect form at this moment. The cry for immediacy is the cry for impossibility. It is a cry without memory or perspective. Immediacy is impossible in a society of human beings. What is possible is to continue patiently to build the structures that permit the development of better justice.

Let us also beware of pat phrases such as "justice delayed is justice denied." Justice delayed is no excuse for antijustice or the destruction of the law system. The fact that particular reforms have not been completely achieved does not justify rejecting legal means—the only hope for lasting achievement.

The demand for equality cannot be converted into a fight for superiority. We must be for equality under the rule of law. We are for freedom *under* law, not freedom *against* the law.

Let us also avoid unreal questions such as whether justice is more important than order or vice versa. Order is the *sine qua non* of the constitutional system if there is to be any possibility for long-term justice based on public consensus.

Flouting the Law

What about the concept of "righteous civil disobedience"? I take it that all men now accept the fact that there can be no justification for violent disobedience under our constitutional system. Is the concept validated when the disobedience is nonviolent? In my opinion this idea has no place in our law society.

Parenthetically, I would suggest that you experts in criminal law consider whether there can be "civil" disobedience where there is a specific intent to disobey the law. Such a specific state of mind is ordinarily treated as the essence of criminality, hence not "civil." Therefore, it seems to me that there is an inherent contradiction in the concept of premeditated, *"righteous"* civil disobedience.

Yet I prefer to base the case on broader grounds. The concept of righteous civil disobedience, I think, is incompatible with the concept of the American legal system. This is particularly axiomatic where this society provides more than any other for orderly change; where every minority—including the minority of one—has been protected by a system of law which provides for orderly process for development and change. I cannot accept the right to disobey where, as here, the law is not static and where, if it is claimed to be oppressive or coercive, many effective channels for change are constantly available. Our courts do not have to apologize for their continued dedication to the liberty of all men. Our legislatures have regularly met the changing times and changing needs of the society with consideration for the unalienable rights of all. Even the federal and state constitutions have been amended. Our law has not only been a guardian of freedom, but the affirmative agent for freedom.

While the idea of civil disobedience may evoke sympathy where the claim is made that the cause is just, once we accept such a doubtful doctrine we legitimatize it for other causes which we might reject. We must be even more careful in the sympathetic case because, in effect, that sets the standard of conduct which then becomes acceptable for cases not as appealing or for groups not as responsible. Thus, we substitute pressure for persuasion and squander the carefully nurtured value of self-restraint and jeopardize the system of law.

The plain fact of human nature is that the organized disobedience of masses stirs up the primitive. This has been true of a soccer crowd and a lynch mob. Psychologically and psychiatrically it is very clear that no man—no matter how well-intentioned—can keep group passions in control.

Disobedience Breeds Disrespect

Civil disobedience is an *ad hoc* device at best, and *ad hoc* measures in a law society are dangerous. Civil disobedience under these circumstances is at best deplorable and at worst destructive.

Specific disobedience breeds disrespect and promotes general disobedience. Our grievances must be settled in the courts and not in the streets. Muscle is no substitute for morality. Civil disobedience is negative, where we require affirmative processes. We must insist that men use their minds and not their biceps. But, while the emphasis must be on the three R's of reason, responsibility, and respect, we cannot accept self-righteousness, complacency, and noninvolvement. We reject hypocritical tokenism. We have an affirmative and daily duty to eliminate discrimination and provide opportunity—full opportunity and meaningful equal justice for all our people.

In an era of social, political, and scientific revolutions—and at a time of accelerating and complex change—we of the law must particularly renew our understanding and improve our articulation of the basic issue of freedom under law and the continuing need to strive for equality and meaningful liberty and justice for all.

Freedom is not some easy gift of nature. The plant of liberty has not grown in profusion in the wilderness of human history. Liberty under law is a fragile flower. It must be nurtured anew by each generation of responsible citizenry. Let but a year of neglect be sanctioned, even *celebrated,* and the jungle of force threatens to recapture the untended garden.

4

Civil Disobedience Is a Christian Act

Duane Heffelbower

Duane Heffelbower is an attorney who recently closed his Reedley, California, practice to become coordinator of Developmental Disabilities Services (West Coast MCC) and to study at Mennonite Brethren Biblical Seminary, Fresno, California.

In this classic viewpoint, Heffelbower argues that civil disobedience is an inherently Christian act, in that Jesus Christ himself used acts of civil disobedience against unjust Roman laws. In going back into the history of civil disobedience in Christianity, Heffelbower brings his argument to modern times, stating that the US and Canadian governments have enshrined civil disobedience as a "valid method of speaking to the government." However, he states, civil disobedience must be conducted according to the "Christian conscience" and to release ourselves from the captivity of unjust legal and economic systems present in our governments.

C hristians live in tension between the demands of the world in which they live and the demands of Christian discipleship. This article will examine the point at which obedience to God and obedience to government clash, and will offer a method of dealing with the conflict.

"The Christian and Civil Disobedience," by Duane Heffelbower, from *Direction*, ©1986, published by Kindred Productions. Used with permission.

For the purpose of this article, "civil disobedience" is defined as:

Purposeful, nonviolent action, or refusal to act, by a Christian who believes such action or inaction is required of him or her in order to be faithful to God, and which s/he knows will be treated by the governing authorities as a violation of law.

This article further assumes a Christian pacifist stance which rejects violence as a means to any end.

Three Scripture passages are generally cited for the proposition that Christians are to obey the government:

Submit yourselves for the Lord's sake to every authority instituted among men: whether to the king, as the supreme authority, or to the governors, who are sent by him to punish those who do wrong and to commend those who do right. For it is God's will that by doing good you should silence the ignorant talk of foolish men (1 Peter 2:13-15 NIV).

Remind the people to be subject to rulers and authorities, to be obedient, to be ready to do whatever is good, to slander no one, to be peaceable and considerate, and to show true humility toward all men (Titus 3:1-2 NIV).

Everyone must submit himself to the governing authorities, for there is no authority except that which God has established. The authorities which exist have been established by God. Consequently, he who rebels against the authority is rebelling against what God has instituted, and those who do so will bring judgment on themselves (Romans 13:1-2 NIV).

A History of Holy Obedience and Civil Disobedience

The tension in which Christians find themselves is shown in Acts 4 when the Sanhedrin orders Peter and John not to teach or speak in the name of Jesus, and they ask whether it is right to obey God or men. Paul was quite willing to use the Roman legal system when he was arrested in Jerusalem rather than be flogged, and was able to witness in new ways because of it. Being a Christian was itself a violation of law in much of the civilized world until Constantine endorsed Christianity. Sixteenth-century Anabaptists violated the law by not baptizing their infants and by rebaptizing adults.

It is also important to remember that before Jesus began to preach the Jews were certainly in tension with their rulers. Josephus, in his *Antiquities of the Jews*, tells the story of Jewish resistance to Pilate's introduction of images of the emperor into Jerusalem. A large number of Jews lay in the courtyard for five days in protest, and when Pilate ordered his soldiers to surround them and threatened slaughter if the Jews did not submit, they instead bared their necks and said slaughter was preferable to the images. Pilate relented.[1]

Historically, the points of tension between Christians and their governments have centered upon either the government's demand that all citizens subscribe to and follow the practices of a state religion or the government's prohibition of Christian practices which are central to the faith. Military service has been a problem for both reasons, since in pre-Constantinian times emperor {25} worship or sacrifice to idols tended to be required of soldiers of Rome and since the early Christians understood that killing was contrary to Jesus' teaching whether done in peace or war. Marcellus the centurion, who was martyred in A.D. 298, objected for both reasons. He is quoted as saying in part:

> I cease from this military service of your emperors, and I scorn to adore your gods of stone and wood, which are deaf and dumb idols. If such is the position of those who render military service that they should be compelled to sacrifice to gods and emperors, then I cast down my vine-staff and belt, I renounce the standards, and I refuse to serve as a soldier . . . I threw down my arms; for it was not seemly that a Christian man, who renders military service to the Lord Christ, should render it also by inflicting earthly injuries.[2]

For Anabaptists of the sixteenth century adult baptism and military service were key points of tension with the government. The *Martyrs Mirror* shows how Christians have responded to demands of the government which directly contradicted their faith. The heroic acts told of in the *Martyrs Mirror* do not seem the same as what we usually call civil disobedience in modern times, but the only real difference is the higher cost to those who defied the government in centuries past.

The concept of civil disobedience was developed by Henry David Thoreau in the 19th century. In the western world emperors did not demand worship, and the concept of civil disobedience was applied to "social issues" such as slavery, child labor, women's suffrage, and prohibition of alcohol. Mahatma Gandhi was influenced by Thoreau's work on civil disobedience. We need to review church history in the light of North American understandings of individualism and personal liberty and remind ourselves that those concepts were not part of the pre-Constantinian world view. Nor were they part of the 16th century world view. Marcellus did not throw down his staff and belt to make a statement about who he was as an individual nor to strike a blow for individual liberty. Marcellus renounced soldiering as being unfaithful to his true Lord. When we talk about Christian civil disobedience we are not talking about Thoreau and his New England Transcendentalism which focused on private conscience as against majority expediency.[3] We are talking about faithfulness to God which transcends all earthly loyalties.

To Test Our Obediences

Nevertheless, the scripture passages quoted at the beginning make it clear that we are to be subject to the governing authorities. How is it that one is subject to government, yet refuses to obey it? That would appear to be a contradiction. John Howard Yoder offers an explanation:

> It is not by accident that the imperative of [Romans] 13:1 is not literally one of *obedience*. The Greek language has good words to denote obedience, in the sense of completely bending one's will and one's actions to the desires of another. What Paul calls for, however, is sub*or*dination. This verb is based on the same root as the *ordering* of the powers by God. Subordination

is significantly different from obedience. The conscientious objector who refuses to do what his government asks him to do, but still remains under the sovereignty of that government and accepts the penalties which it imposes, . . . is being subordinate even though he is not obeying.[4]

It is clear from the New Testament that Jesus' followers did not blindly obey the governments under which they found themselves. Faithfulness to God was first. It is also clear that the sixteenth-century Anabaptists were faithful to God first and the state second. Jesus knew that his followers would be in tension with the authorities. He instructed them:

> You will be handed over to the local councils and flogged in the synagogues. On account of me you will stand before governors and kings as witnesses to them. And the gospel must first be preached to all nations. Whenever you are arrested and brought to trial, do not worry beforehand about what to say. Just say whatever is given you at the time, for it is not you speaking, but the Holy Spirit (Mark 13:9b-11 NIV).

These are hardly the instructions of a leader expecting his followers to *obey* every authority instituted among men. For the sake of the gospel followers of Jesus will refuse to obey men. But, for the Lord's sake, the followers of Jesus will *submit* to every authority instituted among men, and by so doing will bear witness to those authorities. As John Howard Yoder puts it: "We subject ourselves to government because it was in so doing that Jesus revealed and achieved God's victory."[5]

Granting our desire to submit to government, and granting our desire to be faithful, what do we do when we believe the state is asking us to behave contrary to God's will for us? D. Edmond Hiebert offers some initial guidance:

> Peter's condensed instructions [1 Peter 2:13] did not deal with the believer's response whenever government demands that which is contrary to the Christian faith. In Acts 4:19 and 5:29 we have the example of Peter himself concerning the Christian response under such conditions. For the Christian the state is

not the highest authority, and whenever government demands that which is in conflict with the dictates of the conscience enlightened by the Holy Spirit and the Word, then the Christian must obey the Word of God and suffer the results. 'The Church soon learned by bitter experience that there are some things which the state has no right to do, and that therefore the counsel of submission has its limitations: [footnote] But under ordinary circumstances, believers should actively support civil government in its promotion of law and order.[6]

The key here would seem to be a conscience enlightened by the Holy Spirit and the Word. Since Anabaptist Mennonites believe that the Holy Spirit also speaks through the body of believers, this would indicate another test. The Word and the Spirit speaking in concert with the body of believers will tell us when the state has overstepped its bounds and when a Christian must say "no" to the state. But what shape does that holy "no" take?

Looking back at our definition of Christian civil disobedience, we need a way of testing what we do. One commentator has suggested five qualifications on civil disobedience (not necessarily Christian in its motivation): (1) The law opposed is immoral, in conflict with a higher claim; (2) every possible nondisobedient recourse has been exhausted, with the definition of "possible" and "exhausted" being tempered by the situation; (3) the protest is not clandestine; (4) there is a likelihood of success (drawing a distinction between purely personal action taken for conscience sake and the sort of social disobedience which seeks to change society and thus must have its potential bad effects balanced against the good likely to emerge); (5) there is willingness to accept the penalty.[7] Looking more specifically at the church's witness to the state, another commentator finds three additional tests, which also apply to individual Christian witness to the state: (1) The witness must be representative of the church's clear conviction; (2) the witness of the church must be consistent with her own behavior; (3) the church should speak only when she has something to say, rather than feeling obligated to "cover the field."[8] If we follow these suggestions, there is much more likelihood of civil disobedience being truly holy obedience.

Holy Obedience in a North American Democracy

We should also recognize that the current North American governmental systems are set in place with civil disobedience as a valid method of speaking to government. A quotation from the Declaration of Independence of the United States is instructive on this point:

> . . . We hold these truths to be self-evident: That all men are created equal; that they are endowed by their creator with certain unalienable rights; that among these are life, liberty and the pursuit of happiness; that, to secure these rights, governments are instituted among men, deriving their just powers from the consent of the governed; that whenever any form of government becomes destructive of these ends, it is the right of the people to alter or to abolish it and to institute a new government. . . .

While not so blatantly stated, the Canadian Constitution has a similar underlying presumption. In a modern western democracy a good citizen is one who calls the government to account for its actions and who, through the political process, works to make the government better. How does Christian civil disobedience fit into a system where, through the political process, everything is "up for grabs?"

The governmental system of the United States, and, generally speaking, the Canadian situation as well, functions as follows: laws are made by the Congress, implemented by the executive branch, and tested for constitutionality by the courts. The courts also act in a quasi-legislative way when they interpret acts of Congress or the executive as those acts apply to a specific situation.

When the government acts in a way which violates Christian conscience under the tests set out above, Christians have several ways to work with the situation. They can seek legislation which changes that which they abhor, they can use the courts to determine whether the law actually applies to them in the way it seems to, they can use the courts in an effort to overturn the law as being a violation of the Constitution, or they can submit to the government while refusing to obey the law. All of these methods have been used by Mennonites in this century on the issues of conscription and of the paying of taxes which go for war purposes. The Amish have successfully obtained exemption from Social Security by these methods, and the concept of conscientious objection to military service came into existence in this way. What is also true of these instances is that what turned the political tide was the willingness of Christians to do Holy Obedience, and their quiet willingness to go to jail rather than to obey the government. Mennonites active in the fight against conscription have said again and again that it was the willingness of Mennonite boys to go to jail which turned the hearts of the people in government to make possible the exemption of conscientious objectors from military service.

The governments of the United States, Canada and most other countries respect people genuinely motivated by religious belief. It is difficult, however, for persons in government to know when they have met such people. There are so many people touting a wide variety of issues for their own advantage that it is difficult for anyone to distinguish between those who speak from firmly held religious convictions and those who speak only from enlightened self interest. The way to most surely separate the two is by seeing who resorts to Holy Obedience rather than choosing the less costly path of obeying the government. Whether or not this is as it should be does not matter for our purposes here. If cowardice and financial hardship were proper reasons for exclusion from military service there would never be an army. But a person willing to endure greater hardship for the sake of their belief in God's way can be exempted by the government with little risk that most persons will choose that path. Hendrik Berkhof speaks to this idea:

> All resistance and every attack against the gods of this age will
> be unfruitful, unless the church itself *is* resistance and attack,
> unless she demonstrates in her life and fellowship how men can
> live freed from the powers. We can only preach the manifold

wisdom of God to mammon if our life displays that we are joyfully freed from his clutches.[9]

We Christians often find ourselves in a dilemma when we try to love our neighbors as ourselves. So often, as Ronald J. Sider suggests, we think it is more spiritual to operate "ambulances" which pick up the bloody victims of destructive social structures rather than trying to change the structures themselves.[10] In 1975 the General Conference Mennonite church was faced with the question of how to respond to an employee's request that income taxes not be withheld from her wages due to her opposition to paying for war. As part of its process for dealing with the request, the Conference called together a group of its leaders along with other theologians and attorneys to consider the matter in preparation for creating study materials for its congregations. The concluding word of the findings committee of that consultation will serve as our concluding word here:

> It is important for all of us to remember how easily and quickly we can become captives of the system of thought and economics that prevails at present in our society. By God's grace we are called from conformity to the transformation of our lives by the renewal of mind and spirit to know and do the will of God. The potential for good of such obedience is as limitless as God's love and grace, and God's peace will flow from His church like a river to bless the nations.[11]

Notes

1. Flavius Josephus, *Antiquities of the Jews*, in *Josephus, The Complete Works*, trans. by William Whiston (Grand Rapids: Kregel Publications, 1960), p. 379.
2. Cecil John Cadoux, *The Early Christian Attitude to War* (New York: The Seabury Press, 1982), p. 152.
3. Paul Sherman, "Thoreau, Henry David, *Encyclopedia Britannica*, 1969, XXI, 1073-1075.
4. John Howard Yoder, *The Politics of Jesus* (Grand Rapids: William B. Eerdmans Publishing Company, 1972), p. 212.
5. John Howard Yoder, *Politics, supra*, p. 213.
6. D. Edmond Hiebert, *First Peter, An Expositional Commentary* (Chicago: Moody Press, 1984), p. 154.
7. Stephen Charles Mott, *Biblical Ethics and Social Change* (New York: Oxford University Press, 1982), pp. 161-165.

8. John Howard Yoder, *The Christian Witness to the State* (Newton, KS: Faith and Life Press, 1964), p. 21.

9. Hendrik Berkhof, *Christ and the Powers* (Scottdale, PA: Herald Press, 1962), p. 51.

10. Ronald J. Sider, *Rich Christians in an Age of Hunger* (Downers Grove, IL. Inter-Varsity Press, 2d. ed., 1984), p. 192.

11. Consultation on Civil Responsibility, Elkhart, Indiana, June 1-4, 1978, Findings Committee Report. (Typewritten with handwritten alterations.)

5

Christians Must Use Civil Disobedience Against Our Nuclear Security State

Jim Douglass

Jim Douglass is an American author, activist, and Christian theologian. He is the author of JFK and the Unspeakable: Why He Died and Why It Matters.

Douglass begins this viewpoint by stating that the "nuclear security state" is the "greatest evil conceivable." What Douglass is referring to is the United States's position as a country with large stocks of nuclear arms—enough to destroy not only an "enemy" city, but the entire world. Against this great evil, Douglass states that Christians have the moral obligation to resist peacefully. However, he argues, they must not fall into the trap of seeing the world in terms of "good" and "evil," as this is what allowed nuclear arms proliferation in the first place. Thus, a correct use of civil disobedience becomes similar to reflective prayer.

One way of seeing jail today is to regard it as the monastery. In a society preparing for nuclear war and ignoring its poor, jail is an appropriate setting in which to give one's life to prayer. In a nation which has legalized preparation for the destruction of all life on earth, going to jail for peace—through nonviolent civil disobedience—can be seen as prayer. In reflecting today on the Lord's Prayer, I think that going to jail as a way of saying "thy

"Civil Disobedience as Prayer," by Jim Douglass, Red Letter Christians, February 4, 2013. Reprinted by permission.

kingdom come, thy will be done" may be the most basic prayer we can offer in the nuclear security state. Because we have accepted the greatest evil conceivable as a substitute for divine security, we have become a nation of blasphemers. The nuclear state is blasphemous by definition. As members of such a nation, we need to pray for the freedom to do God's will by noncooperating with the ultimate evil it is preparing. Civil disobedience done in a loving spirit is itself that kind of prayer.

On the other hand, civil disobedience can be done in a way that, while apparently noncooperating with nuclear war, ends up cooperating with an illusion that underlies nuclear war. In any attitude of resistance to the state there is a kind of demonic underside, power turned upside down, which wishes to gain the upper hand. Civil disobedience which is not done as prayer is especially vulnerable to its underside.

A simple truth at the root of nonviolence is that we can't change an evil or an injustice from the outside. Thomas Merton stated this truth at the conclusion of one of his last books, *Mystics and Zen Masters,* as a critique of "nonviolence" as it is understood by its proponents in the Western world. Merton questioned "the Western acceptance of a 'will to transform others' in terms of one's own prophetic insight accepted as a norm of pure justice." He asked: "Is there not an 'optical illusion' in an eschatological spirit which, however much it may appeal to *agape,* seeks only to transform persons and social structures *from the outside?*" Here we arrive at a basic principle, one might almost say an ontology of nonviolence, which requires further investigation.

Nonviolent noncooperation with the greatest evil in history is still, according to Merton's insight, a possible way into illusion, a more subtle form of the same illusion that we encounter behind the nuclear buildup. Even in nonviolent resistance, unless we accept deeply the spirit of nonviolence, we can end up waging our own form of war and contributing to the conclusion we seek to overcome. Because the evil we resist is so great, we are inclined to overlook an illusion inherent in our own position, the will to transform others from the outside.

If one understands civil disobedience as an assertion of individual conscience over against the evil or injustice of the state, the temptation to seek an "outside solution" is already present. Conscience against the state sounds like a spiritually based or "inside solution." We are, after all, stating our willingness in conscience to go to jail at the hands of the state that threatens an unparalleled evil. But our conscience set off against the nuclear state takes an external view of people acting on behalf of that state. And ultimately such a view externalizes our own conscience.

In the acts of civil disobedience that I have done, I have never met "the state." In terms of my own ambition, that has been disappointing. I have met only people, such as police, judges, and jail guards, who cooperate (and sometimes noncooperate) with the evil of nuclear war in complex and often puzzling ways. I have never met a person who embodies that state of nuclear war. In their nuances of character, police, judges, and guards come from the same stew of humanity as do people who do civil disobedience.

A spiritually based nonviolence, one that truly seeks change from within, has to engage deeply the spirits of both sides of a conflict. Civil disobedience as an act of conscience against the state tends to focus exclusively on our own conscience as a source of change. Yet in the act of civil disobedience we meet particular people like ourselves, not "the state," and the most enduring thing we can achieve through such an act is, in the end, our relationship to the people we touch and who touch us. Our hope should not be for any strategic victories over such representatives of the state but rather loving, nonviolence relationships with them in the midst of our arrests, trials, and prison sentences. The danger of seeing civil disobedience as an assertion of conscience over against the evil of the state is that it may get confused into an assertion against these particular people so that we may never really see our relationship to them as primary. Making friends with our opponents—in the

Pentagon or in Al Qaeda—is our greatest hope of overcoming nuclear war.

A more fundamental question suggested by Merton is: Who is this "I," this self, that is doing the act of conscience in civil disobedience? If civil disobedience accentuates, or heightens, this sense of self—if it gives it a sense of power—is that necessarily a good thing? Civil disobedience is often referred to today as a way of empowering its participants. For socially powerless people, nonviolent civil disobedience can be a profoundly liberating way out of bondage, as one part of a larger revolution. But empowerment can also be used to cover a heightened sense of an individual self that may be a step into further bondage.

We who see ourselves as peacemakers—and don't we all?—would be deeply shocked if we could see the extent to which we act personally for war, not only in our more obvious faults, but even in our very peacemaking. Our intentions and actions for peace lead to war if they are based on a false self and its illusions. If the purpose of civil disobedience is to "empower" such a self, it is a personal act of war.

The nuclear arms race summarizes the history of a false, violent self—of many such false selves magnified in national egos—in an inconceivable evil. What the nuclear crisis says to us, as nothing else in history could, is that the empowering of a false self creates a crisis which has no solution, only transformation. We can't *solve* an arms race based on enormous national illusions, illusions which both exploit and protect an emptiness at the center of millions of lives. Those illusions can only be cracked open to the truth and fear and emptiness at the core of each national pride, then revealed as truly reconcilable with their apparent opposites in the consciousness of another people.

Civil disobedience for the sake of empowering a false self serves as the warring nation state on a smaller scale. Civil disobedience as that kind of empowerment is an attempt to solve one's problems and frustrations by externalizing them in a theater in which innocence confronts the evil of the nuclear state. But we are not innocent.

The greatest treason, as T.S. Eliot points out in *Murder in the Cathedral*, is to do the right deed for the wrong reason. Civil disobedience in response to the greatest evil in history, done to empower a self which can't face its own emptiness, is the right deed for the wrong reason. Because of its motivation, it may also twist itself into the wrong deed. An ego-empowering act of civil disobedience will in the end empower both the self and the nuclear state, which, while tactically at odds, are spiritually in agreement. Such resistance, like the state itself, asserts power in order to cover a void. Civil disobedience, like war, can be used to mask the emptiness of a false self.

Civil disobedience as prayer is not an assertion of individual conscience over the evil of the state. Protesting against something for which we ourselves are profoundly responsible is a futile exercise in hypocrisy. The evil of nuclear war is not external to us, so that it can be isolated in the state or in the Nuclear Train loaded with hydrogen bombs. The nature of the evil lies in our cooperation with it. What Merton is suggesting is that as we cease cooperating in one way with that evil, our well-hidden tendency is to begin cooperating with it more intensely and more blindly in another way, defining the evil in a way external to us, which deepens and hardens its actual presence in ourselves.

The power of the evil of nuclear war is nothing more than the power of our cooperation with it. There is no evil exclusively out there, over us. The evil is much more subtle than that. This is why it continues to exist. When we cease cooperating with evil at its source in ourselves, it ceases to exist. When we accept responsibility for nuclear war in the hidden dimensions of our own complicity, we will experience the miracle of seeing the Nuclear Train stop and the arms race end. To paraphrase Harry Truman, the Bomb stops here. Civil disobedience as prayer is not an assertion of self over an illusion but an acceptance of God's loving will because of our responsibility for evil: Not my will but thine be done. The prayer of the gospels like the prayer of Gandhi is at its heart an acceptance of what we don't want: the acceptance of our suffering out of love. Jesus and Gandhi are precise about what is meant by God's will in a world of suffering. Gandhi in summing up Jesus' life said, "Living Christ means a living cross, without it life is a living death."

To be nonviolent means to accept our suffering out of love. The evil which causes suffering is an evil whose source is more deeply interior to ourselves than we have begun to understand. The prayer of civil disobedience which says, *"Not my will but thine be done"*—by sending us to death or to that sign of death which is jail—is a recognition that in truth we belong there, and that we will in any event ultimately find ourselves there. Civil disobedience as prayer is not an act of defiance but an act of obedience to a deeper, interior will within us and within the world which is capable of transforming the world. "Thy kingdom come, thy will be done." To live out the kingdom of God through such an action is to live in a loving relationship to our brothers and sisters in the police, in courts, and in jails, recognizing God's presence in each of us. It is also to accept responsibility for an evil which is ours: As we are, so is the nuclear state.

The two most violent places I've ever been in my life have been the Strategic Weapons Facility Pacific (SWFPAC), at the heart of Seattle's Trident submarine base, where nuclear weapons are stored, and the Los Angeles County Jail, where people are stored a the heart of LA. I went to SWFPAC in order to pray for peace and forgiveness standing in front of enormous concrete bunkers, the tombs of humankind, a prayer which took me in turn to the LA County Jail (on the way to a more permanent prison) where ten thousand people are kept in tombs. The deepest experiences of peace that I have had have been in these same terrible places.

I believe that a suffering God continually calls us to be in such places for the sake of peace and justice. I believe that the kingdom of God is realized there. Civil disobedience as prayer is a way into that kingdom.

6

Environmental Activists Have a Legal Obligation to Use Civil Disobedience

Jeremy Brecher

Jeremy Brecher is a historian and the cofounder of the Labor Network for Sustainability. His book, Climate Insurgency: A Strategy for Survival *was published in 2015.*

Jeremy Brecher is a well-known environmental activist who has used civil disobedience routinely in his fight for more environmental controls. In this viewpoint, Brecher goes deep into a historical legal analysis of res communs, *or "common things," in order to argue that civil disobedience is an expected and necessary action to take in the light of the destruction of our public good. This means that it is a legal dictate to protect "the commons"—including the environment we all share—and that those who use civil disobedience against the destruction of the commons are actually fulfilling a legal obligation.*

Two years ago I was among more than a thousand people who committed civil disobedience at the White House to oppose the building of the Keystone XL pipeline. Since then many more have been arrested around the country, often blocking the actual pathway along which the Keystone XL is being constructed. Nearly 70,000 people have vowed to risk arrest if the State Department recommends that the president approve the pipeline.

"Civil Disobedience as Law Enforcement," by Jeremy Brecher, Waging Nonviolence, August 14, 2013. http://wagingnonviolence.org/feature/civil-disobedience-as-law-enforcement/. Licensed under CC BY 4.0 International.

All along I believed that these actions were justified, even though they meant breaking the law. After all, leading NASA climate change specialist Jim Hansen says that the Alberta tar sands, which the pipeline will carry, "must be left in the ground" because "if the tar sands are thrown into the mix it is essentially game over" for a viable planet.

Since being arrested at the White House, my perspective on the nature of such actions has changed. After learning about a fundamental principle of American law known as the public trust doctrine, I have come to believe that the U.S. government and other governments around the world are violating their own most fundamental responsibilities to their own people when they allow fossil fuel producers and users to devastate the earth's atmosphere with greenhouse gases.

Governments will no doubt continue to treat protesters who block pipelines, coal mines and power plants as criminals. But such governments come into court with dirty hands, stained by their dereliction of the duty to protect the common inheritance of their own people.

Res communes

The public trust doctrine has roots and analogues in ancient societies from Europe to East Asia to Africa, and from Islamic to Native American cultures. It was codified in the *Institutes of Justinian*, issued by the Roman Emperor in 535 A.D. The Justinian code defined the concept of *res communes* (common things): "By the law of nature these things are common to mankind — the air, running water, the sea and consequently the shores of the sea." The right of fishing in the sea from the shore "belongs to all men." The Justinian code distinguished such *res communes* from *res publicae*, things which belong to the state.

Based on the Justinian Code's protection of *res communes*, governments have long served as trustees for rights held in common. In American law this role is defined by the public trust doctrine, under which the state serves as trustee on behalf of the present and future generations of its citizens. Even if the state holds title to a given resource, the public is the "beneficial owner." As trustee, the state has a fiduciary duty to the owner—a legal duty to act solely in the owners' interest. This principle is accepted today in both common law and civil law systems in countries ranging from South Africa to the Philippines and from the United States to India.

International law, furthermore, recognizes regions that lie outside of the political reach of any one nation state—specifically, the high seas, the atmosphere, Antarctica and outer space— as "global commons" governed by the principle that they are "the common heritage of humankind." But there has been no effective vehicle for asserting our right not to have our common heritage destroyed.

Suing for an inheritance

In a series of suits and petitions on behalf of young people in 2011, the Atmospheric Trust Litigation Project brought legal actions to all 50 U.S. states and the federal government demanding that they fulfill their public trust obligation to protect the atmosphere as a common property. Sixteen-year-old Alec Loorz, founder of Kids v. Global Warming and lead plaintiff in the federal lawsuit, said, "The government has a legal responsibility to protect the future for our children. So we are demanding that they recognize the atmosphere as a commons that needs to be preserved, and commit to a plan to reduce emissions to a safe level."

The suits seek declaratory judgment applying the public trust doctrine to the earth's atmosphere. They ask courts to issue injunctions ordering federal and state governments to reduce carbon emissions to fulfill their duty to protect it. Similar suits are projected for countries around the world. While the courts have turned down some of these suits, in 2012 a federal district court ordered that a case brought in New Mexico go forward.

There is precedent supporting the public trust doctrine in the United States. The U.S. Supreme Court decided, in a leading public trust case at the end of the 19th century, that the state's power resulted from "common ownership" of the public trust asset. That power, the decision stated, should be exercised as "a trust for the benefit of the people," not as a "prerogative for the advantage of the government, as distinct from the people." The ownership is "that of the people in their united sovereignty."

The trustee has an active duty of vigilance to prevent decay or "waste"—permanent damage to the asset. If the asset is wasted in the interest of one generation of beneficiaries over future generations, it is in effect an act of generational theft.

When a trust asset crosses the boundaries of sovereign governments, all sovereigns with jurisdiction over the natural territory of the asset have legitimate property claims to the resource. Thus, all nations on Earth are "co-tenant trustees" of the global atmosphere. As co-tenants they have an undivided right to possess the property. But they also have a duty not to allow the waste of the common property.

As compelling as the logic of such an argument may be, it is easy to imagine that many American courts will refuse to force governments to meet their obligations. In a brief to dismiss the Kansas suit, lawyers called the claim "a child's wish for a better world," which is not something a court can do much about. "No order issued by the District Court of Shawnee County can hold back global warming, any more than King Canute could order the tide to recede."

The sad fact is that virtually all the governments on earth—and their legal systems—are deeply corrupted by the very forces that profit from destroying the global commons. These governments exercise illegitimate power without regard to their obligations to those they claim to represent, let alone to the future generations to whom they are mere trustees.

Civil disobedience, reconsidered

Protecting the global commons is not just a matter for governments. The failure of governments to protect the global commons is currently driving the climate protection movement to turn to mass civil disobedience, as witnessed by the campaigns against the Keystone XL pipeline, mountaintop-removal coal mining and coal-fired power plants. Looked at from the perspective of the global commons, however, these actions are far from disobedient. Indeed, they embody the effort of people around the world to assert their right and responsibility to protect the global commons. They show people acting in an emergency situation on an evident necessity. They represent people stepping in to provide law enforcement where corrupt and illegitimate governments have failed to meet their responsibility to do so.

Legal rationales have played a critical role in many nonviolent movements. They strengthen participants by lending a sense of clarity that they are not promoting personal opinions by criminal means but rather performing a public duty. And they strengthen a movement's appeal to the broader society by presenting action not as wanton lawbreaking but as an effort to rectify governments and institutions that are themselves in violation of the law.

For the civil rights movement, the Constitution's guarantee of equal rights meant that sit-inners and freedom riders were not criminals but rather upholders of Constitutional law. For war resisters during U.S. wars from Vietnam to Iraq, the international law that since the Nuremberg trials has forbidden war crimes has defined civil disobedience as an obligation under international law. For those who took part in the nonviolent revolution that overthrew communism in Poland, their struggle was not criminal sedition, but an effort to implement the international human and labor rights laws ratified by their own government.

The legal obligation of governments to protect the public trust can play a role similar to governments' obligation to protect human rights and eschew war crimes. Those who perpetrate climate change, and those who allow them to do so, should not be able to claim that the law is on their side. Those who blockade coal-fired power plants or sit down at the White House to protest the Keystone XL pipeline can—and should—insist that they are simply exercising their right and responsibility to protect the atmospheric commons they own along with all of present and future humankind.

Future climate protesters can proudly proclaim that they are actually climate protectors, upholding the law, not violating it. Nobody should expect American judges to start acquitting protesters on public trust grounds any time soon. But juries that try climate protesters should keep in mind that they have the right and the responsibility to acquit those they believe have violated no just law.

7

Students Must Find Ways to Take Non-Violent Action Against Climate Change

Harvard University Center for the Environment

The Harvard University Center for the Environment (HUCE) encourages research and education about the environment and the importance of environmental protections and draws its strength from Harvard University faculty and students.

Based on scientific research, global warming is rising at an increasingly worrisome rate. While there are those who would argue against the human cause of this, few scientists and environmentalists would argue against these nonpartisan findings. In this viewpoint, Harvard students and alumni speak about the actions they have taken in order to stop this devastating trend. In particular, the article delves into nonviolent actions that students can and have successfully taken, such as divestment, in order to make their voices heard against the oil industry and its power in government. However, these actions have not always been uncontroversial—particularly among the Harvard community.

The world is on track to experience an average increase in air temperature of four to six degrees Celsius over pre-industrial levels, according to recent analysis by the International Energy Agency. Such warming would pose severe threats to human society: displacement by rising seas of millions of people who live

"Social Movements and Climate Change," Harvard University Center for the Environment, June 17, 2013. Reprinted by permission.

along vulnerable coastlines; increasing frequency and intensity of storms; diminished agricultural harvests; declines in biodiversity; desertification; and more severe droughts and floods, among its effects.

Carbon-capping legislation, which most climate experts and economists say will be necessary (if not sufficient) if we are to avert the most dire scenarios, and which stalled in Congress in 2010—is unlikely to be revived soon. But the political fight is just beginning.

Harvard faculty, students, and alumni are actively considering how the climate change issue will move forward. Many do this through their scholarship and teaching, but some are getting more involved, from shaping climate policy inside the White House to engaging in civil disobedience outside its front gate. Their work confronts a wide range of questions. What is the role of social movements in addressing a challenge as complex and daunting as climate change? What kinds of specific actions will be effective in swaying decision-makers, polluters and the public? What mix of tactics, targets and articulated goals are most likely to break political gridlock on the issue, and make a real difference in everyone's stated goal: dramatically reducing emissions of carbon dioxide and other greenhouse pollutants? And most importantly, what should be the goal of activism? That question is at the center of an impending battle for the heart and soul of the environmental movement.

Morality as Motivation

On the climate issue, the problem is that "urgency is not felt by many people," says Marshall Ganz, a senior lecturer at Harvard Kennedy School. "But one thing that movements do is come up with ways to make the important urgent."

Ganz speaks from experience. He left Harvard during his junior year to work with the civil rights movement in Mississippi in 1964. He went on to work with Cesar Chavez and the United Farm Workers for 16 years, before eventually returning to Harvard to complete a Ph.D. in sociology. One of the lessons he draws from his decades working in and studying social movements is that moral urgency—a sense of injustice, or even anger—is often needed to move individuals to act. This is often accompanied by hope, or the sense of the plausible, the possible. Action of this kind may produce change in the participants themselves, as well as in the world around them.

"If you look at the core of any social movement there are highly committed people who are ready to take risks," he says. "It's not just about passing a law—at heart they are movements of moral reform. Take the Harvard living wage campaign back in 2001, when the students sat in the president's office and said, 'We're not going to leave until it gets dealt with.'" This had the effect of turning what the students saw as a morally urgent problem into a practically urgent problem for decision-makers to resolve.

"How to make that cosmic sense of urgency immediately felt is one of the challenges of this (climate) movement," Ganz continues. "That's where civil disobedience and that kind of activity comes in—it's a way of saying we're not going to cooperate until you address this need."

Ganz met recently with a group of law school students seeking advice on the campaign to press Harvard's administration to divest from fossil fuel companies. He says he supports the students' efforts on the merits of their moral argument, but also as a means to stir up and "mobilize the kind of movement it will take to make broader and deeper change."

"There is a very strong generational dynamic to this whole thing," Ganz says. "Generation change is one of the great drivers of cultural and political change. Bill McKibben ['82] gets that, which is why he has this focus on divestment: give the rising generation a strategic focus." But some scholars question whether McKibben is chasing the wrong targets.

How to Build a Movement

McKibben, a journalist by training and temperament, is arguably the most prominent climate activist on the planet. In 1989, he wrote the first book on climate change for a popular audience,

The End of Nature. After decades of covering climate science—and observing the collective failure to create commensurate solutions—in 2008 he co-founded 350.org with students at Middlebury College, where he is a scholar in residence. Their explicit goal was to build a grassroots movement to fight climate change.

McKibben has become the leader of a fast-growing movement that he dubs the "Fossil Fuel Resistance." Like Ganz, he sees a need for proven tactics such as civil disobedience and demonstrations. In October 2009, prior to the international climate negotiations in Copenhagen, 350.org orchestrated simultaneous rallies in 181 countries—possibly the largest coordinated protest in history. In August 2011, in one of the largest civil disobedience actions in decades, McKibben was arrested along with more than 1200 others in front of the White House during a protest of the proposed Keystone XL pipeline, which would ferry oil extracted from the tar sands of Alberta to the Gulf of Mexico for export. He spent three days in jail.

The tempo of McKibben's campaigning picked up last summer, after he wrote an article in *Rolling Stone* magazine titled "Global Warming's Terrifying New Math". In it he described recent research outlining how, if the world's governments are serious about their commitments to staying under the two degree Celsius warming threshold, then 80 percent of the estimated carbon reserves held by fossil fuel companies around the world will need to stay in the ground, and out of the atmosphere. The story went viral, prompting McKibben and fellow activists to go on a barnstorming tour to spread this message in packed lecture halls and theaters across the country.

Their message resonates with students, at least. Since last fall, fossil fuel divestment campaigns have sprung up on more than 300 college campuses. On April 11, almost 200 people gathered in Harvard Yard to deliver a petition calling on Harvard's administration to divest the University's $31 billion endowment—the nation's largest—from fossil fuel companies. Their goal wasn't only to get the Harvard Corporation to rethink its investment priorities, but to make a statement, and loudly.

"It was incredible," recalled Chloe Maxmin '15, co-coordinator of Divest Harvard, the day after the rally. "We have so many voices calling for divestment. Alumni were emailing President Faust yesterday as we were rallying outside, and faculty and the chaplain at Memorial Church were with us."

Maxmin and her fellow demonstrators persuaded Secretary of the University and Vice President Marc Goodheart to come outside and publicly accept the 1300 signatures on a petition that didn't mince words: "Although Harvard has been a national leader in institutional sustainability, we find it contradictory and self-defeating that Harvard invests its endowment in companies that threaten the future of its students and life on Earth as we know it." Many of Maxmin's peers seem to agree: in a November referendum held by the Harvard Undergraduate Council, 72 percent of participating students voted to support divestment. "On some level it's very intuitive," Maxmin says. "It's wrong to be investing in these corporations because their business model is incompatible with the future of our generation."

But while faculty members laud students for civic engagement, they do not necessarily embrace the aims of the current protest. "It is wonderful to see student activism arise surrounding climate change," says Hooper professor of geology Daniel Schrag, who directs the Harvard Center for the Environment (HUCE).

"But what does it mean when students push Harvard to divest from fossil fuel companies, but then fly home on airplanes and drive around in cars fueled by petroleum, communicating on their iPhones using electricity generated from coal and natural gas? We need a profound change in the energy systems and infrastructure that underlie our society, and Harvard's role is to develop new technologies and ways of implementing them, and most of all to educate our students who will lead the world through this transition."

These future leaders, some of whom are involved in groups now at the forefront of climate activism, are leveraging their voices through the use of social media such as Twitter and other low-cost and lightning-quick tools for reaching vast numbers of people. "It's a good thing that we have the Internet—a globally linked way to communicate—just as we hit our first truly global problem," says McKibben. "It can't be the only way we proceed (emailing each other petitions has its limits of effectiveness) but it is a huge help. It helps spread the news of older, time-honored tactics like civil disobedience."

Still, if climate campaigners are to build a truly broad coalition that can compete with the political clout of the fossil fuel industry, he acknowledges that no amount of Tweeting can take the place of the patient, painstaking work of outreach to grassroots organizations: "Working with partners across the progressive spectrum always takes lots of talk, and lots of respect in all directions."

Meanwhile, the Keystone protests gathered diverse support, from college students to Nebraska ranchers to Appalachians opposed to mountaintop-removal coal mining. McKibben compares this burgeoning movement to Occupy Wall Street: they are more interested in creating a national groundswell than in counting votes in the Senate or getting engaged in specific policy fights. "Before we have any real chance," McKibben says, "we have to change the mood around this issue, building a real movement."

Forging a Broader Coalition

Theda Skocpol, Thomas professor of government and sociology, has been studying political and social movements for much of her career. She recently conducted a thorough post-mortem on the failed push for cap-and-trade legislation in Congress in 2009 and 2010. Her analysis concludes that mainstream environmental organizations were overly focused on making an "insider deal" with business interests, with little grassroots support.

"To build leverage on Congress," she writes, "and to push back effectively against elite and populist anti-environmental forces, global warming reformers must mobilize broad, popularly rooted support for carbon-capping measures that have something concrete to offer not just to big corporate players, but also to ordinary American citizens and to local and state groups."

Skocpol is focused on what can shift lawmakers' thinking on the costs and benefits of climate action. Her answer: strong constituencies for change. "I'm asking people to think not about the science or the urgency of the moral crisis, but the politics," she said in an interview. "And that's not easy to separate."

"I don't think people are clear-eyed about any of this," she continued, referring to "bipartisan fantasies" that the big environmental groups brought to negotiations. "There is romanticism on the far left, too, that all you have to have is some demonstrations, the Occupy Wall Street fantasy"—one which McKibben seems to embrace.

In preparation for the next round of battles over carbon-pricing or -capping legislation, Skocpol sees potential in persuading both Republican and Democratic moderates that this can be a winning issue for them. "You do need to go well beyond the network of organizations that already think of themselves as environmentalists," she says. "Environmentalism remains a very upper middle class, coastal movement."

Skocpol advocates better-organized outreach to church groups, labor unions, community organizations and groups like the League of Women's Voters. "I think one has to cast a wide net and prepare to be surprised." She further argues that any successful alliance pushing climate legislation will have to be built around specific policy proposals that do not impose undue economic burdens on the public. "People have to realize that policy directions and coalitions go together," she says. "My research shows that the bottom four-fifths of Americans have not seen real income growth, and that creates a real dilemma any time you're doing something that raises costs. And frankly, it will raise costs."

Choosing the Right Targets

What are the requisite ingredients of successful social movements? Several scholars identify key components: passionate participants driven by a sense of moral urgency; careful organization; diverse coalitions; and the identification of effective—and sensible—points of leverage.

On that latter point, Joseph Aldy, an assistant professor of public policy at HKS and former special assistant to President Obama for energy and environment, would encourage activists to focus on those actors blocking action in Congress.

In 2008, the presidential nominees of both major parties agreed that climate change was a serious problem, and both expressed support for cap-and- trade-based solutions. But after the failure of climate legislation in the Senate in 2010, "cap-and-trade" became a dirty word in Washington, largely thanks to aggressive lobbying by fossil fuel interests and outspoken opposition from the Tea Party faction of the Republican Party. "We have too many people who think the earth is just flat again," Aldy says, referring to Republican lawmakers and their supporters who deny climate change is an urgent, or even real, problem. Social movements need "to mobilize people to impose a political cost on people who say there is no such thing as climate change."

"It's a little peculiar to be targeting those who are already trying to do what they can to tackle this issue," he says in reference to McKibben's Washington, D.C. Keystone protests. Citing President Obama's achievements on fuel efficiency standards and other fronts, he says his former boss has done more than any previous president to reduce emissions. Protesters' energy would be better spent, he suggests, targeting those politicians who "still don't think this is an important issue at all." Likewise, Aldy thinks activists should target the energy industry more carefully. "Keystone is a very transparent measure of success from a social movement standpoint," he says, in that the pipeline will either be approved or denied. "But does it affect global climate in the next twenty years? I don't think so."

William Hogan, Plank professor of global energy policy at HKS, agrees that approval of Keystone wouldn't make big a difference in terms of global carbon dioxide emissions. He is concerned that the "theater" of fights over Keystone and divestment makes it more difficult to have an honest conversation about the costs and benefits of specific policies that would make a difference in global emissions. "The worldview of the people arguing for divestment and so forth often seems to be disconnected from the facts," he says. "I'm always fundamentally concerned about people who say things that are not true: 'Keystone is the end of the world. Game over.' That's just silly."

"I'm in favor of taxing all energy-related emissions and putting a price on them," he says. "A lot of people would be prepared to pay five percent of GDP" to stay within safe limits on atmospheric carbon levels, "but not everybody would." He laments that environmental groups' current tack leaves little room for a "nuanced conversation" about the critical question of "how much we're willing to pay" to slow climate change.

William Clark, Brooks professor of international science, public policy and human development at HKS, concedes that activists like McKibben "have a great moral advantage in this, in that they are doing something instead of simply wringing their hands." He also acknowledges the potential symbolic power of campaigns to make a moral statement about the urgency of reigning in our consumption of fossil fuels. But he shares his colleagues' skepticism that divestment is the best way to go about it. "It's not enough to say, 'This is something we can get people to rally around.'"

"There's somewhere between a lack of clarity and a muddle in terms of what the divestment movement is trying to accomplish," he says. "Divestiture isn't a goal, it's a means to some end."

If fossil fuel production stopped tomorrow, he points out, society as we know it would collapse. As individuals, we demand fossil fuels, he says. And the world economy is built on them.

Clark appreciates the need to build momentum on the issue. But he points to Occupy Wall Street as a cautionary example of a movement that had some impact on the national conversation, and then faded for lack of clear objectives. "If you look back at the civil rights movement, one of the pieces of genius was managing to keep the outrage and moral focus of the movement tied to relatively small, achievable steps." Clark would like to see, instead of a "negative, 'stop things' movement," more emphasis on making proactive, positive investments: "We can preferentially direct our investments into areas with an energy and climate agenda."

If opposition is "needed to rally people," Clark continues, "then let's target the very worst, obstructionist actors, the ones undermining science and spreading disinformation. I would say, look, we're a university, we may well have different perspectives as individuals over the right mix of fuels, the right degree of government intervention. But some individuals and firms out there are undermining the center of our existence as a university: respect for the importance and power of efforts to get closer to the truth. Target them."

McKibben has heard such criticisms before, and given his goal of "changing the mood" around the issue, he thinks targeting the Keystone pipeline and investments in fossil fuel companies might offer symbolic, rabble-rousing value that goes beyond the precise amount of carbon kept out of the atmosphere. The cognitive dissonance of the investment positions of institutions such as Harvard, he says, are fair game.

"I don't think we're radical at all," he says. "All we want is a world that works the way it did when we were born. We're conservatives. It's oil companies—and the institutions like Harvard willing to profit from them—that are radicals, willing to change the chemical composition of the atmosphere. I don't think there's ever been a more radical act in human history."

A Rational Path?

So where does the climate movement go from here?

As Marshall Ganz likes to point out, all social movements are "unpredictable, messy, contentious." Debate over how to push for climate solutions will no doubt continue, and will likely take new, unanticipated directions—but only if these nascent stirrings of energy are sustained through what is sure to be a decades-long struggle to transform the very underpinnings of the modern global economy.

In 1964, Ganz picketed Harvard administrators to demand they divest from Mississippi Light and Power Company. That effort failed, but "a lot of us who cut our teeth challenging them to divest…went on to play a role in the movement." Whether or not Maxmin and her colleagues are successful in their push for divestment, there will be a need for continued engagement in the coming years, much as Ganz went on to work for decades to advance civil and labor rights. Says Schrag, "Student activism is exactly what we need, and the exact demands seem less important than the fact that they are actually mobilizing and demanding change. So I applaud their protests to gain attention. I just don't think the University should follow their specific demands."

What is clear is that the University will continue to be a "place of contention," said Ganz at a recent event in Sanders Theatre. Reasonable people can disagree on the path forward, on the choice of tactics, targets, even goals. But simply doing nothing is looking increasingly unreasonable.

8

The Time Is Now to Use Mass Action to Stop Crimes Against the Environment

Kara Moses

Kara Moses is a freelance writer, journalist, editor and activist who also currently serves as environment editor for Red Pepper *magazine.*

In this viewpoint, Kara Moses focuses on the power that citizens versus corporations hold, particularly in regard to the environment. Moses powerfully argues that corporations have long committed "crimes against the environment without retribution" while regular citizens, like her coalminer grandfather, have suffered. The world has now reached a turning point, Moses states, where more people are aware of the environmental threat and are ready to take action— including participating in protests that shut down coal mines. While environmental activists often risk being arrested while taking part in such mass actions, Moses feels that now is the time for these activists to grab the world's attention and to finally make a lasting change.

Right now, thousands of people are taking direct action as part of a global wave of protests against the biggest fossil fuel infrastructure projects across the world. We kicked off earlier this month by shutting down the UK's largest opencast coal mine in south Wales.

Last Sunday, around 1,000 people closed the world's largest coal-exporting port in Newcastle, Australia and other bold actions

"Civil Disobedience is the Only Way Left to Fight Climate Change," Kara Moses, Common Dreams, 5/13/2016. ©Guardian News & Media Ltd 2017. Reprinted by permission.

are happening at power stations, oil refineries, pipelines and mines everywhere from the Philippines, Brazil and the US, to Nigeria, Germany and India.

This is just the start of the promised escalation after the Paris agreement, and the largest ever act of civil disobedience in the history of the environmental movement. World governments may have agreed to keep warming to 1.5C, but it's up to us to keep fossil fuels in the ground.

With so many governments still dependent on a fossil fuel economy, they can't be relied upon to make the radical change required in the time we need to make it. In the 21 years it took them to agree a (non-binding, inadequate) climate agreement, emissions soared. It's now up to us to now hold them to account, turn words into action and challenge the power and legitimacy of the fossil fuel industry with mass disobedience.

It is unjust that corporations and governments can commit crimes against the planet and society without retribution, while those fighting to prevent such crimes are punished, murdered and incarcerated. But the number of people willing to challenge this is growing. And if we really want climate justice, protest in the pursuit of this must be normalised; we must support rather than denounce those willing to put themselves on the line, since we all benefit from their actions. Not everyone is in a position to take civil disobedience, but we can all get behind it.

Many of the changes that need to be made to tackle climate change would also improve the quality of life for the majority of people on the planet—from allowing people in Beijing to go outside without wearing pollution masks, to creating good jobs for millions.

Mining companies argue that their operations provide vital jobs for local people. But the fossil fuel industry cannot offer secure jobs when it is crumbling (despite the trillions it receives in public subsidies while support for renewables is being pulled). With massive divestment, falling prices, a global climate deal, growing global resistance and increasing scientific evidence about their effects, the demise of the industry is inevitable.

These jobs are not only insecure, but often dangerous. My only memories of my coal miner grandad are of him lying in bed coughing and in pain with a back injury caused at work. The effects of his job continued long after the mine closed and he was made redundant: the respiratory illness that killed him and his brothers was caused by inhaling toxic air from the mine—the same toxic air that communities unfortunate enough to live near a site of fossil fuel extraction or burning have to breathe.

Corporate fossil fuel extraction also leads to local communities dependent on a finite resource, and at the mercy of a corporation whose primary interests are profit. When the oil runs dry or the coal runs out, the company makes its exit, leaving behind all of the pollution and none of the wealth. The area my family lived in, once a thriving community when coal was plentiful, is now a place of high unemployment, social decay and few opportunities.

Renewables can offer not only secure, long-term jobs that are safer and less dependent on specific sites of extraction, but also the opportunity for democratic ownership of energy and sustainable communities. The choice between clean, safe, democratic and sustainable energy/jobs or dirty, dangerous and undemocratic energy/jobs is a no-brainer. We have the technology right now to make the transition to a zero-carbon Britain—the barriers are not technological but political.

To overcome those political barriers, we need to reclaim our power—both in terms of who has power over our lives, and how we power our lives. And as 2017 is said to be the year when the door to reach two degrees closes forever, now is the time to do it. This year must be the year of mass climate disobedience.

9

Pro-Life Activists Can and Should Use Civil Disobedience Against Abortion

Francis J. Beckwith

Francis J. Beckwith, PhD., is associate professor of philosophy, culture, and law, and W. Howard Hoffman Scholar, Trinity Graduate School, Trinity International University (Deerfield, IL), California Campus, and senior research fellow, Nevada Policy Research Institute. His books include Politically Correct Death: Answering the Arguments for Abortion Rights *(Baker, 1993),* Matters of Life and Death: Calm Answers to Tough Questions about Abortion and Euthanasia *(Baker, 1991), and* The Abortion Controversy: A Reader *(Jones & Bartlett, 1994).*

In this viewpoint, Francis J. Beckwith argues that pro-life activists can and should use civil disobedience if they feel abortion is morally wrong. Beckwith draws context both from Martin Luther King Jr.'s fight for civil rights and biblical passages. He systematically addresses objections that those who are against pro-life civil disobedience might have in order to strengthen his argument. However, while Beckwtih states that civil disobedience in this case is morally justified, it is not morally obligatory in his view. This means that pro-lifers should reflect on whether or not civil disobedience is practical and useful to their aims.

"Civil Disobedience and Abortion: A Modern Defense," by Francis J. Beckwith, Christian Research Institute, www.equip.org. Reprinted by permission.

Morally reflective people have wrestled with the question of whether civil disobedience is ever morally justified, and if so, under what circumstances? [1] Throughout history there have been cases of civil disobedience that seem morally justified, including: the early Christian church's refusal to obey the government's command not to preach the gospel (Acts 4); Martin Luther King, Jr.'s refusal to obey racially discriminating laws;[2] and Christians' violation of religiously oppressive laws when smuggling Bibles and doing missionary work.

Many pro-lifers who peacefully block abortion clinics defend civil disobedience from a theological/biblical perspective, and some of their critics thoughtfully argue against them from that perspective as well. I maintain that pro-lifers have a right to violate anti-trespassing laws in order to rescue unborn children. I do not contend, however, that pro-lifers have a moral obligation to do so, since it would be physically impossible as well as entail significant personal risk to save every oppressed person—born or unborn—by breaking the law.[3] Moreover, I believe that prudential considerations—those having to do with whether rescuing as a strategy will do greater harm than good in changing minds and laws—may well lead pro-lifers to avoid civil disobedience altogether during this stage of the abortion controversy in North America.

My position differs from that of Randall Terry, the founder of Operation Rescue (OR), the pro-life group that has given high visibility to pro-life civil disobedience. Terry argues that Christians are obligated to violate the law.[4] My position also differs from certain pro-life critics of Terry, such as Norman Geisler and John and Paul Feinberg, who argue that as the current law exists people have no right to engage in pro-life civil disobedience.[5]

> Henry David Thoreau (1817-1862) published a lecture entitled "Resistance to Civil Government" in 1849. He argued that there is a higher law than the civil law, and that the higher law must be obeyed even if a penalty ensues. Thoreau's "resistance" pertained to the government's endorsement of slavery and its "imperialist war" against Mexico.

Mahatma Gandhi (1869-1948) developed the practice of nonviolent civil disobedience which ultimately forced Great Britain to grant independence to India in 1947.

Martin Luther King, Jr. (1929-1968) was America's most visible civil rights leader from 1955 until his assassination in April, 1968 in Memphis, Tennessee. He advocated Ghandian nonviolent civil disobedience as a means of bringing about social change. He was awarded the Nobel Prize for Peace in 1964.

Randall Terry is the founder and director of Operation Rescue, a nationally organized coalition of pro-life pastors and laypeople that stages sit-ins around abortion clinics in an attempt to save the lives of unborn children. Terry and his supporters believe Christians are obligated to engage in nonviolent civil disobedience as a means of putting an end to abortion.

Defending Pro-life Civil Disobedience

There are many biblical instances of divinely approved civil disobedience.[6] In Exodus 1:15-22 Pharaoh commanded the midwives to slay every male Hebrew baby. But Hebrew midwives Shiprah and Puah "feared God and did not do what the king of Egypt had told them to do; they let the boys live" (v. 17, NIV). As a result "God was kind to the midwives and the people increased and became even more numerous. And because the midwives feared God, he gave them families of their own" (vv. 20-21).

In 1 Kings 18:4 wicked queen Jezebel "was killing off the LORD's prophets." In defiance of her orders the prophet Obadiah "had taken a hundred prophets and hidden them in two caves... and had supplied them with food and water" (v. 4). Although Scripture does not explicitly approve of Obadiah's act, the context and manner of the Bible's presentation implies that God condoned it (see vv. 13-15).

In Joshua 2:1-14 Rahab saved the lives of two Hebrew spies by hiding them from soldiers who were searching for them. Randy Alcorn points out that "the spies had no legal right to be in Jericho, while the soldiers had every legal right to apprehend them."[7] Other instances of divinely approved civil disobedience can be found in Exodus 5, Daniel 3 and 6, Acts 4, and Revelation 12-13.

These and other biblical cases of justified civil disobedience seem to have the following factors in common: (1) the state commands the believer to do something contrary to the Word of God; (2) the command is disobeyed; and (3) there is explicit or implicit divine approval of the refusal to obey the state.

Since the Bible permits or commands Christians to disobey the law only when the state commands them to do evil or not to do good (Acts 5:28-29), some opponents argue that pro-life civil disobedience is wrong because the state does not compel pro-life Christians to abort their unborn children or to participate in abortions. This argument does not succeed for at least two reasons.

First, by forbidding the rescuers to exercise Christ's command to "love your neighbor as yourself" (Matt. 22:39), the government is in fact compelling pro-life Christians to do evil (or at least not to do good). Pro-life Christians believe the unborn child is their neighbor and to rescue that child from certain death is a good thing.

Second, this objection fails if one believes that those who broke the law when hiding Jews from the Holocaust did a good thing. Based on the reasoning of those who oppose pro-life civil disobedience, those who rescued Jews from the Holocaust were wrong since the state was not compelling most of them to kill a Jew or to work in a concentration camp.

Objections

To better understand my view, consider a few objections to pro-life civil disobedience. Since it is impossible in the allotted space to address every objection in the abortion literature,[8] I have chosen three that are the most forceful and popular.

Objection 1: The tactics of certain groups involved in civil disobedience will lead to violence against clinics and doctors, since anything can be justified to "save lives."

There are at least three problems with this argument. First, this objection commits the "slippery-slope" fallacy. It occurs when a person believes that if a certain thing is allowed, it will eventually lead to something bad or far worse. For example, if I were to argue that elementary schools should not ban fifth-graders from reading hard-core pornography because it would eventually lead to banning good literature, I would be committing the slippery-slope fallacy. I would be making the mistake of assuming that there are no distinctions between forms of literature and that we cannot make rational judgments about such matters.

When arguing against the rescuer, the person who commits this fallacy mistakenly assumes that because something might lead to something bad or far worse, it must lead to something bad or far worse. If this reasoning were correct, however, then no action would ever be justified, since it is possible that any action might (in a broad logical sense) lead to something that is undesirable.

This objection incorrectly assumes that the pro-lifer cannot make distinctions between degrees of law-breaking, and that once one allows for peaceful civil disobedience, revolution must follow. The opponent to pro-life civil disobedience has not proven that the civilly disobedient pro-lifer is incapable of providing compelling reasons not to employ violence.[9]

Second, this objection apparently assumes that some rescuers may believe that the end (saving unborn children) justifies the means (including violence), but this assumption seems unwarranted. The rescuers' view is simply that the command to save lives is greater than the command not to trespass. Therefore, it is not necessarily true that the rescuers believe they have the option of using violence whenever they think it may achieve their end.

For example, AIDS activists may believe it is their duty to stop the spread of AIDS. But it would not follow that they would be required to kill every person who is currently diagnosed with HIV or AIDS, even though that would achieve their ends. AIDS activists and pro-life activists do not hold their positions in a moral vacuum; both groups hold to certain other values (i.e., respect for life, the social order, laws, and so forth) that also play a part in their moral decision-making.

Third, even if the rescuers' position were consistent with the use of violence, this would not mean a rescuer would be morally required to engage in such activity. That is to say, rescuers could grant to their objector that they are morally justified in blowing up a clinic (if they are certain beyond a reasonable doubt that no innocent persons would be harmed) as well as attacking a physician who is about to, or is in the process of, killing an unborn child. Rescuers, however, could argue that out of prudential judgment there is no reason to resort to such tactics. Simply because something is morally permissible does not mean it is prudent to do it. Just because I can do something does not mean I must do it. Consequently, even if the use of force were morally justified, prudential judgment indicates that in the current stage of the abortion debate it would be severely counterproductive.

Objection 2: Since spiritual death is worse than physical death, rescuers should also block the entrances to churches that lead people to spiritual death.

Problems with this objection can best be illustrated by the following example: Suppose one had to choose between stopping one of the following two fathers. Father A is taking his son to the woodshed to kill him with a 44-magnum handgun, but only after an hour of torturing him by covering his body with battery acid. Father B is taking his son to the First Church of the False God, where they will attend Sunday service and return home. Even though spiritual death is ultimately worse than physical death, it seems obvious that the rational person would choose to stop Father A, based on two considerations.

First, physical death and spiritual death are fundamentally different. Just as in the case of Father A, the physical death in abortion is inflicted on someone by another and is irreversible. By contrast, spiritual death is self-inflicted (people choose to reject God) and can be reversible prior to physical death.

Second, one prevents physical death differently than one prevents spiritual death. One cannot prevent the spiritual death of another by blocking the entrances to churches. People choose to reject the Lord apart from whether or not they will enter a building. One can only hope to prevent the spiritual death of others by telling them the truth about the Lord and praying for them. Consequently, the child who is led to a false church by his or her parent will ultimately have the opportunity to make a choice for himself or herself after reaching the age of accountability. On the other hand, one can prevent an abortion (physical death) by blocking the entrances to an abortion clinic.

Objection 3: Rescuing makes the pro-life movement look bad and divides the movement.

This is a prudential judgment, not a moral argument. Rescuing may hurt the pro-life movement in terms of popularity and group unity, but it may still be morally justified. Prudential judgments and considerations should never be underestimated, for they are important to political strategy. But they are not decisive in moral judgment. For example, just as giving money to a homeless person may be imprudent (that person may buy whiskey), rescuing may be imprudent as well (it may undermine the long-term political goals of the pro-life movement). Yet both acts may be morally permissible.[10]

Conclusion

It seems that pro-life civil disobedience is morally justified from a biblical perspective. When we look at the Bible, we find that it allows for the violation of a law when—whether directly or indirectly—it prohibits one from obeying a command of God. Since pro-life Christians are required by the enforcement of trespassing laws not to love their unborn neighbors, the law indirectly commands Christians not to obey Jesus' command to love one's neighbor as oneself. Meanwhile, the objections to this view are not compelling. In addition, since pro-life civil disobedience is not morally obligatory, the question confronting the pro-life movement is whether it is a prudent thing to do. The leadership of those groups that engage in pro-life civil disobedience must answer this serious and important question.

Notes

1. See Randy Alcorn, Is Rescuing Right? (Downers Grove, IL: InterVarsity Press, 1990); John Feinberg and Paul Feinberg, Ethics in a Brave New World (Wheaton, IL: Crossway Books, 1993), 91-98; Martin Luther King, Jr., "Letter from the Birmingham Jail," The Right Thing to Do: Basic Readings in Moral Philosophy, ed. James Rachels (New York: Random House, 1989), 236-53; Randall Terry, Operation Rescue (Springdale, PA: Whitaker, 1988); Ernest Van Den Haag, "The Dilemma of Civil Disobedience," Philosophy: The Quest for Truth, ed. Louis P. Pojman (Belmont, CA: Wadsworth, 1989), 433-42; and John Rawls, "The Justification of Civil Disobedience," The Right Thing to Do, 254-70.

2. King.

3. They are called supererogatory acts -- acts in which one has a right to engage but not an obligation since they involve great personal risk. For more on this subject, see Hadley Arkes, First Things: An Inquiry into the First Principles of Morals and Justice (Princeton, NJ: Princeton University Press, 1986), 288-308.

4. Terry, 99-111.

5. Norman L. Geisler, Christian Ethics: Options and Issues (Grand Rapids: Baker Book House, 1989), 239-56; and Feinberg and Feinberg, 91-98.

6. For an excellent overview of the biblical passages, see Alcorn, 4-56.

7. Ibid., 42.

8. Some of the strongest objections to pro-life civil disobedience can be found in Geisler, 239-56; and Feinberg and Feinberg, 91-98.

9. See the recent symposium on this issue: "Killing Abortionists: A Symposium," First Things: A Monthly Journal of Religion and Public Life (December 1994): 24-31.

10. John and Paul Feinberg do an excellent job of weighing these prudential considerations in Ethics in a Brave New World, 97-98.

10

Civil Disobedience Must Be Used According to Martin Luther King Jr.'s Principles

John Dear

John Dear is a Catholic priest and Christian pacifist. He has been arrested over seventy-five times while employing civil disobedience against war, injustice, and the use of nuclear weapons. He has been nominated for the Nobel Peace Prize several times throughout his life.

Drawing on Martin Luther King Jr.'s use of non-violent action in the face of racial injustice, priest and activist John Dear takes a Christian standpoint on the use and methods of civil disobedience. Dear focuses on King's six steps for non–violent action, and draws on the need for education before action, personal commitment, and negotiations during the process, with reconciliation as the end goal. Dear does not state, as in the above article, whether or not civil disobedience should be used or not used for any particular issue or view. Rather, he focuses on the processes and techniques of a Christian-based civil disobedience in the face of any form of discrimination or injustice.

To mark Dr. Martin Luther King Jr.'s birthday, I've been reflecting on the principles of nonviolence that he learned during the historic yearlong bus boycott in Montgomery, Ala.

After Rosa Parks refused to sit in the back of the bus, broke the segregation law and was arrested on Dec. 1, 1955, the African-

"What Martin Luther King Jr. Can Teach Us About Nonviolence," by John Dear, *National Catholic Reporter*, January 17, 2012. Reprinted by permission National Catholic Reporter Publishing Company. NCRonline.org.

American leadership in Montgomery famously chose young Rev. Dr. Martin Luther King Jr. to lead their campaign.

He was an unknown quantity. Certainly no one expected him to emerge as a Moses-like tower of strength. No one imagined he would invoke Gandhi's method of nonviolent resistance in Christian language as the basis for the boycott. But from day one, he was a force to be reckoned with.

With the help of Bayard Rustin and Glenn Smiley of the Fellowship of Reconciliation, Dr. King articulated a methodology of nonviolence that still rings true. It's an ethic of nonviolent resistance that's also a strategy of hope, which can help us today in the thousands of Montgomery-like movements around the world, including the Occupy movements and the ongoing Arab Spring movements.

Dr. King outlined his way of nonviolence in his 1958 account of the Montgomery movement, *Stride Toward Freedom* (published by Harper and Row, pp. 83–88). There, he tells the story of the movement and his own personal journey, then offers six basic points for nonviolence. Dr. King lived and taught these essential ingredients of active nonviolence until the day he died. (For an excellent commentary on them, I recommend *Roots of Resistance: The Nonviolent Ethic of Martin Luther King, Jr.*, by William D. Watley, Valley Forge, Judson Press, 1985.)

These fundamental principles, along with his six steps for nonviolent action, make up Dr. King's "to do" list:

Nonviolence is the way of the strong.

Nonviolence is not for the cowardly, the weak, the passive, the apathetic or the fearful. "Nonviolent resistance does resist," he wrote. "It is not a method of stagnant passivity. While the nonviolent resister is passive in the sense that he is not physically aggressive toward his opponent, his mind and emotions are always active, constantly seeking to persuade his opponent that he is wrong. The method is passive physically, but strongly active spiritually. It is not passive non-resistance to evil; it is active nonviolent resistance to evil."

The goal of nonviolence is redemption and reconciliation.

"Nonviolence does not seek to defeat or humiliate the opponent but to win friendship and understanding," King teaches. "The nonviolent resister must often express his protest through noncooperation or boycotts, but he realizes that these are not ends themselves; they are merely means to awaken a sense of moral shame in the opponent....The aftermath of nonviolence is the creation of the beloved community, while the aftermath of violence is tragic bitterness."

Nonviolence seeks to defeat evil, not people.

Nonviolence is directed "against forces of evil rather than against persons who happen to be doing the evil. It is evil that the nonviolent resister seeks to defeat, not the persons victimized by evil."

"Not only did King depersonalize the goal of nonviolence by defining it in terms of reconciliation rather than the defeat of the opponent, but he also depersonalized the target of the nonviolent resister's attack," Watley writes. "The opponent for King is a symbol of a greater evil. ... The evildoers were victims of evil as much as were the individuals and communities that the evildoers oppressed."

In this thinking, King echoes St. Paul's admonition that our struggle is ultimately not against particular people but systems —"the principalities and powers."

Nonviolence includes a willingness to accept suffering without retaliation, to accept blows from the opponent without striking back.

"The nonviolent resister is willing to accept violence if necessary, but never to inflict it," King writes. "Unearned suffering is redemptive. Suffering, the nonviolent resister realizes, has tremendous educational and transforming possibilities."

That's a tough pill to swallow, but King insists there is power in the acceptance of unearned suffering love, as the nonviolent resister Jesus showed on Calvary and Dr. King himself showed in his own life and death.

In *Stride Toward Freedom*, King urged nonviolent resisters to paraphrase Gandhi and say:

> We will match your capacity to inflict suffering with our capacity to endure suffering. We will meet your physical force with soul force. We will not hate you, but we cannot in all good conscience obey your unjust laws. Do to us what you will and we will still love you. Bomb our homes and threaten our children; send your hooded perpetrators of violence into our communicates and drag us out on some wayside road, beating us and leaving us half dead, and we will still love you. But we will soon wear you down by our capacity to suffer. And in winning our freedom we will so appeal to your heart and conscience that we will win you in the process. (p. 194)

Nonviolence avoids not only external physical violence but also internal violence of spirit. It practices agape/love in action.

"The nonviolent resister not only refuses to shoot his opponent; he also refuses to hate him. At the center of nonviolence stands the principle of love."

Cutting off the chain of hate "can only be done by projecting the ethic of love to the center of our lives." Love means "understanding, redemptive goodwill toward all people."

For King, this agape/love is the power of God working within us, Watley explains. That is why King could exhort us to the highest possible, unconditional, universal, all-encompassing love. King the preacher believed God worked through us when we used the weapon of nonviolent love.

Nonviolence is based on the conviction that the universe is on the side of justice.

"The believer in nonviolence has deep faith in the future," King writes. "He knows that in his struggle for justice he has cosmic companionship. There is a creative force in this universe that works to bring the disconnected aspects of reality into a harmonious whole." King's philosophy, spirituality, theology and methodology were rooted in hope.

These core principles explain why, for King, nonviolence was "the morally excellent way." As he boldly expanded his campaign from Montgomery to Atlanta, Albany and eventually Birmingham, he demonstrated six basic steps of nonviolent action that could be applied to any nonviolent movement for social change. As explained in *Active Nonviolence* (Vol. I, ed. by Richard Deats, *The Fellowship of Reconciliation*, 1991), every campaign of nonviolence usually undergoes these basic stages toward justice, and they are worth our consideration:

Information gathering. We need to do our homework and learn everything we can about the issue, problem or injustice so we become experts on the topic.

Education. Then we do our best to inform everyone, including the opposition, about the issue and use every form of media to educate the population.

Personal commitment. As we engage in the public struggle for nonviolent social change, we renew ourselves every day in the way of nonviolence. As we learn that nonviolent struggles take time, we commit ourselves to the long haul and do the hard inner work necessary to center ourselves in love and wisdom and prepare ourselves for the possibility of rejection, arrest, jail or suffering for the cause.

Negotiations. We try to engage our opponents, point out their injustice, propose a way out and resolve the situation, using win-win strategies.

Direct action. If necessary, we take nonviolent direct action to force the opponent to deal with the issue and resolve the injustice, using nonviolent means such as boycotts, marches, rallies, petitions, voting campaigns and civil disobedience.

Reconciliation. In the end, we try to reconcile with our opponents, even to become their friends (as Nelson Mandela demonstrated in South Africa), so that we all can begin to heal and move closer to the vision of the "beloved community."

Dr. King's principles and methodology of nonviolence outline a path to social change that still holds true. In his strategy, the ends are already present in the means; the seeds of a peaceful outcome can be found in our peaceful means. He argues that if we resist injustice through steadfast nonviolence and build a movement along these lines, we take the high ground as demonstrated in the lives of Jesus and Gandhi and can redeem society and create a new culture of nonviolence.

"May all who suffer oppression in this world reject the self-defeating method of retaliatory violence and choose the method that seeks to redeem," Dr. King concluded. "Through using this method wisely and courageously we will emerge from the bleak and desolate midnight of 'man's inhumanity to man' into the bright daybreak of freedom and justice." Amen.

11

Civil Disobedience Plays an Important Role in Democracy

Kayla Starr

Kayla Starr is a writer for Civilliberties.org.

Kayla Starr begins this viewpoint with a historical overview of past uses of civil disobedience that have formed the foundation of American democracy. In particular, Starr focuses on "non-cooperation" as a particular action that can be taken during civil disobedience. Non-cooperation means peaceful resistance in the face of police action or arrest, such as refusing arrest by going limp or refusing food once in jail. Many activists have used these techniques in the past to great effect, although Starr notes that non-cooperation is a personal choice and does not need to be used by all who practice civil disobedience more broadly.

Civil Disobedience is the act of disobeying a law on grounds of moral or political principle. It is an attempt to influence society to accept a dissenting point of view. Although it usually uses tactics of nonviolence, it is more than mere passive resistance since it often takes active forms such as illegal street demonstrations or peaceful occupations of premises. The classic treatise on this topic is Henry David Thoreau's "On the Duty of Civil Disobedience," which states that when a person's conscience and the laws clash, that person must follow his or her conscience. The stress on personal

"The Role of Civil Disobedience in Democracy," by Kayla Starr, National War Tax Resistance Coordinating Committee. Reprinted by permission.

conscience and on the need to act now rather than to wait for legal change are recurring elements in civil disobedience movements. The U.S. Bill of Rights asserts that the authority of a government is derived from the consent of the governed, and whenever any form of government becomes destructive, it is the right and duty of the people to alter or abolish it.

Throughout the history of the U.S., civil disobedience has played a significant role in many of the social reforms that we all take for granted today. Some of the most well known of these are:

1) The Boston Tea Party—citizens of the colony of Massachusetts trespassed on a British ship and threw its cargo (tea from England) overboard, rather than be forced to pay taxes without representation to Britain. This was one of the many acts of civil disobedience leading to the War for Independence, establishing the United States of America as a sovereign state.

2) Anti-war movements have been a part of U.S. history since Thoreau went to jail for refusing to participate in the U.S. war against Mexico in 1849. More recent examples were the nationwide protests against the war in Viet Nam, U.S involvement in Nicaragua and Central America, and the Gulf War. Actions have included refusal to pay for war, refusal to enlist in the military, occupation of draft centers, sit-ins, blockades, peace camps, and refusal to allow military recruiters on high school and college campuses.

3) The Women's Suffrage Movement lasted from 1848 until 1920, when thousands of courageous women marched in the streets, endured hunger strikes, and submitted to arrest and jail in order to gain the right to vote.

4) Abolition of slavery—including Harriet Tubman's underground railway, giving sanctuary, and other actions which helped to end slavery.

5) The introduction of labor laws and unions. Sit-down strikes organized by the IWW, and CIO free speech confrontations led to the eradication of child labor and improved working conditions, established the 40-hour work week and improved job security and benefits.

6) The Civil Rights Movement, led by Martin Luther King, Jr. and others, included sit-ins and illegal marches which weakened segregation in the south.

7) The Anti-Nuclear Movement, stimulated by people like Karen Silkwood and the Three Mile Island nuclear power accident, organized citizens throughout the country into direct action affinity groups, with consensus decision making and Gandhian nonviolence as its core. Massive acts of civil disobedience took place at nuclear power facilities across the country, followed by worldwide protests against first-strike nuclear weapons, occupying military bases, maintaining peace camps, interfering with manufacture and transport of nuclear bombs and devices, marching, sitting in, blockading and otherwise disrupting business as usual at nuclear sites.

8) Environmental and forest demonstrations, with acts of civil disobedience such as sit-ins, blockades, tree sits and forest occupations, have emerged in the last decade, prompted by the continuing mass clear cuts and destruction of the forest ecosystem and widespread environmental consequences.

In all of these struggles, citizens had reached the conclusion that the legal means for addressing their concerns had not worked. They had tried petitioning, lobbying, writing letters, going to court, voting for candidates that represented their interests, legal protest, and still their views were ignored.

In each of these movements, the protesters were compelled by deep moral convictions. Their distress was strong enough to motivate them to go against the grain, to sacrifice personal comfort, to face unknown danger, to give up their freedom and risk going to jail. Their love of truth and justice drove them to action. Many, but not all, of those committing civil disobedience in the last two decades have been trained in Gandhian nonviolence philosophy and tactics.

Non-cooperation is used by some protesters during civil disobedience actions. Non-cooperation may include going limp, refusal to give information at booking, fasting and refusal to particpate in court proceedings.

Gandhi, who profoundly influenced nonviolent disobedience movements in the 20th century, stated that "Non-cooperation with evil is as much a duty as cooperation with good." Non-cooperation is not intended as a hostile act against police officers and jail guards. An understood theoretical basis is that nonviolent protest draws its strength from open confrontation and non-cooperation, i.e., civil disobedience. We retain as much power as we refuse to relinquish to the government. Non-cooperation is a form of resistance that is used to reaffirm our position that we are not criminals and that we are taking positive steps toward freeing the world of oppression and environmental suicide.

The decision to non-cooperate is a difficult choice to make, since it subjects those who choose it to greater possibilities for pain and punishment, and many times is misunderstood by law enforcement. In addition, it poses a dilemma for protesters who would prefer to communicate with the arresting officer, making it more difficult to communicate while being dragged across the ground.

Reasons some protesters choose non-cooperation:

1) Moral conviction: It would be wrong to be an accomplice to a procedure that supports what is morally unacceptable.

2) To increase the likelihood that all protesters are treated equally: Refusing to give names so that everyone committing the same act will be treated equally and fairly in jail and in sentencing. Refusing citation, bail, fines

or probation keeps protesters together, increasing the potential for collective bargaining.

3) To extend the action: Going limp at arrest impedes the removal of the protesters, prolonging the disruption of business as usual.

4) To demonstrate that the criminal justice system is part of the problem: It may be a corporation that is damaging the environment, jeopardizing all our lives and our children's future, but it is the criminal justice system that is legitimizing and supporting it.

Civil disobedience is often an effective means of changing laws and protecting liberties. It also embodies an important moral concept that there are times when law and justice do not coincide and that to obey the law at such times can be an abdication of ethical responsibility. The choice of civil disobedience and non-cooperation is not for everyone. We all choose to do what feels right to us personally. However, it is hoped that this article will make such a choice more understandable to those who have wondered about this form of protest.

12

Civil Disobedience Will Always Be Necessary, but We Must Keep It Relevant

Philip Wight

Philip Wight is a Rose and Irving Crown Fellow and a PhD candidate at Brandeis University. He studies contemporary American intellectual and environmental history.

In this viewpoint, Wight takes the example of thirty-six environmental activists who protested the Keystone XL pipeline in Boston in 2013. During this protest, security officials refused to arrest these protesters— essentially blocking their ability to commit civil disobedience. In the face of such a response to civil disobedience, Wight asks if it is still a useful technique for use by environmental activists and others. He bases his argument on historians and other experts in the field, such as Lewis Perry, who argue that, while civil disobedience is always necessary, activists must continue to update their practices in order to keep them relevant.

I t wasn't the rain that stopped 36 people from getting arrested last month at a Keystone XL pipeline protest in Boston—it was likely State Department officials. After protesters blocked the front entrance to the Tip O'Neil Federal Building, security officials refused to arrest anyone. Intent on committing civil disobedience, however, the protesters moved and blocked another entrance—all

"Has Civil Disobedience Become Too Predictable?" by Philip Wight, Waging Nonviolence, November 5, 2013. http://wagingnonviolence.org/feature/civil-disobedience-become-predictable/. Licensed under CC BY 4.0 International.

while organizers announced with a bullhorn that the group was breaking federal law. But the security officials remained unwilling to accommodate the protesters. Eventually the situation dissipated and all 36 walked away without incident.

This recent experience begs the question: Has civil disobedience lost its effectiveness?

As intellectual historian Lewis Perry details in his new book *Civil Disobedience: An American Tradition*, last month's Keystone XL protest was far from the first time civil disobedience has failed to provoke its desired reaction. In 1961, the civil rights movement used civil disobedience in attempts to desegregate Albany, Ga. However, Sheriff Laurie Pritchett had read Martin Luther King, Jr.'s memoir of the Montgomery bus boycott and understood that nonviolence was especially effective when it evoked a violent response. Publicly, the sheriff met "nonviolence with nonviolence" and denied the movement much-needed media attention. Later, Pritchett even bailed King out from jail to undercut his publicity. Fortunately for the movement, there were far more Bull Connors —the infamous safety commissioner who unleashed attack dogs and fire hoses on civil rights protesters in Birmingham, Ala.— than Laurie Pritchetts.

Examining the "practice, justification, and criticism of civil disobedience in the United States," Perry claims his work is the first to analyze the grand narrative of extralegal protest. As a sympathetic historian, he hopes illuminating the subject's origins and history will allow readers to grapple with the profound moral, political and legal dimensions of civil disobedience.

Although Perry admits civil disobedience is "an odd and elusive concept," he is firm to distinguish it from forms of violent resistance or less direct actions like boycotts. "We cannot understand civil disobedience," he contends, "if we generalize it to include all forms of resistance, day-to-day or extraordinary." Like most respected theorists of dissent, Perry concludes civil disobedience entails a commitment to nonviolence, openness, respect for the law and subjecting oneself to the legal consequences. However, he does explore the most prominent fault lines: fleeing arrest, property destruction, self-defense and coercion.

Tracing the earliest examples of disobedience, Perry argues that the tradition originated when personal conscience—informed by "religious conviction"—was challenged by the power of the state. This delicate dance resulted in a "paradoxical feeling of wanting to respect the law and institutions of civil society while being unable to acquiesce in or ignore immoralities in those laws and institutions." As a middle ground between acquiescence and rebellion, Perry argues civil disobedience emerged as "conservative law-breaking," which "actually intensified respect for law." Its widespread use transformed civil disobedience into an "extension of public life," evolving from a tactic primarily concerned with private conscience in the 19th century to one "increasingly linked to power" in the 20th century.

For students of nonviolence, Perry's scholarship offers both familiar and unexplored examples. His accounts of the civil rights movement and 1960s student protests are excellent but well-traveled territory. Perry excels when he explores those confrontations that have evaded historians for far too long. His first chapter details the case of Samuel Worcester, a missionary sent to "civilize" the Cherokee and was later arrested resisting their removal. Perry then restores the forgotten agency of black abolitionists, who straddled the line between obedience in striving for citizenship and disobedience in resisting slavery. He continues tracing the tradition through an overdue analysis of civil disobedience during the struggle for women's suffrage and an investigation of extralegal dissent in the pro-life movement.

There is much to recommend in Perry's scholarship, especially for active practitioners of nonviolent direct action. While Civil Disobedience offers a useful history for activists, readers should be warned it is not a quick read or one that elicits easy lessons. But broad parallels can be made—most importantly, as creativity is the lifeblood of nonviolence, thinking about past controversies can inspire activists in the present.

Perry's scholarship affirms that nonviolent direct action has more in common with conflict than peace. Gandhi especially respected the discipline, coordination and preparation of soldiers. This lesson is quite relevant for climate justice advocates in light of evidence raised by Josh Fox's disturbing new documentary film Gasland II. At a natural gas conference, a hidden camera reveals a fracking industry representative encouraging the use of U.S. Army counterinsurgency tactics against the populace of resisting towns. Clearly, the fossil fuel companies know the extraction of every last hydrocarbon means war. Therefore, activists must prepare to meet them on the battlefield of nonviolent conflict.

In both the abolition and the civil rights movements, effective use of nonviolent direct action emboldened advocates of slavery and Jim Crow. The current campaign against the fossil fuel regime reveals a similar recalcitrance. Despite increasing evidence and activism, the industry has doubled-down on denial and anti-renewable lobbying. As Has-Werner Sinn argues in The Green Paradox: A Supply-Side Approach to Global Warming, efforts by environmentalists have, perversely, accelerated the extraction of fossil fuels—with companies scrambling to extract as much as possible before social pressure blocks the carbon spigot. But rather than let this news dishearten their resolve, climate activists should heed the famous message—which Perry recalls—of an Industrial Workers of the World activist on death row: "Don't mourn ... organize!"

The biggest lesson offered by Perry's scholarship concerns the dilemma Keystone XL opponents faced last month in Boston. He notes, "Every day's newspaper includes an example of someone invoking a right of civil disobedience." Although legitimate, Perry observes, it has also become circumscribed. And therein lies the great dilemma of civil disobedience: Its ubiquitous and orthodox practice is undermining its effectiveness.

However imperfect the parallel, the predictable deployment of civil disobedience at the Boston sit-in last month may have precipitated something similar to Pritchett's outmaneuver of

King and the civil rights movement. Organizers informed the State Department days beforehand and allowed federal officials to strategize a defensive posture. The sit-in was formulaic—a textbook action that might have only had a few minutes in the limelight. As an exceedingly civil protest, the action fell short of unbalancing authorities and provoking an embarrassing reaction.

A. Phillip Randolph—the famous civil rights leader, astute strategist of nonviolence and architect of the 1963 March on Washington—sought to avoid these kinds of actions. Instead, he counseled that nonviolent direct action must be "revolutionary, unusual, extraordinary, dramatic and drastic in order to be effective in placing the cause of a minority into the mainstream of national and international opinion."

There are, of course, examples of such innovative dissent within the climate movement. Tim DeChristopher's bold disruption of a corrupt oil and gas lease auction in 2008 saved thousands of acres of Utah public lands and invigorated the climate justice movement. Similarly, Ken Ward and Jay O'Hara's blockade of a bulk coal freighter—with the small fishing vessel Henry David T. —precipitated a grassroots movement this summer that influenced the decision to shut down a Massachusetts coal-fired power plant. Then there's the recent interference of coal trains in Montana, the disruption of tar sands extraction in Utah, and the valiant efforts of the Tar Sands Blockade in Texas and Oklahoma—not to mention the efforts of indigenous peoples reasserting their land rights. Each has shown how a new generation of activists can evolve time-tested tactics and directly target fossil fuel infrastructure.

After reading Perry's *Civil Disobedience*, the challenge facing the climate movement is clear: It must make civil disobedience increasingly assertive and imaginative, and it must avoid descending into mindless permissiveness or counter-cultural antics. Practitioners must remember that disobedience is a means to an end — not an end in itself. Disobedience must remain radical—in the literal meaning of the word, "striking at the root"—while also appealing to a broad audience and encouraging solidarity. At best, actions should evoke empathy and stir the public's conscience.

The paradox and dilemmas of civil disobedience will always remain, but so will the imperative for citizens to challenge unjust laws and promote the public welfare. As Perry argues, the atrocities of the last century affirm "a defense of civil disobedience as obligatory for citizens" and accentuate "the urgency of individual moral choice not to be a bystander."

In short, civil disobedience will always remain necessary, but it falls to practitioners and theorists keep it relevant.

13

War Tax Resistance Works Against Unjust Wars

David Gross

David Gross is the author of 99 Tactics of Successful Tax Resistance Campaigns. *He has actively protested the wars in Iraq and Afghanistan through resisting payments of taxes.*

In this viewpoint, David Gross focuses on tax resistance as a relevant and useful avenue of civil disobedience. Gross profiles the War Tax Resisters Penalty Fund, an organization that has protected US war tax resisters from the Internal Revenue Service (IRS) since 1982. Interviewing fund steering committee member Peter Smith, he states that few war tax resisters have faced severe penalties and that it is a viable action for pacifists and activists. Smith, himself, argues convincingly that he can't understand why anti-war activists don't use this technique more convincingly. "It just seems so obvious," Smith states. "If you're against war you shouldn't pay for it."

The thing about the 1 percent is that we outnumber them. They don't have enough jail cells to lock us all down. They ought to be terrified. But what they lack in numbers they make up for in craftiness. They don't have to go after all of us: If they target a few, the rest lose courage and fall back in line.

"Protecting War Tax Resistance Strengthens Antiwar Movement," by David Gross, Waging Nonviolence, February 11, 2016. http://wagingnonviolence.org/feature/protecting-war-tax-resistance-strengthens-antiwar-movement/. Licensed under CC BY 4.0 International.

But this only works if we fail to organize creatively. With a well-run mutual aid program, if the government targets someone, the rest of us make sure that person doesn't bear the brunt alone. One example is the War Tax Resisters Penalty Fund, which has been protecting U.S. war tax resisters from the IRS since 1982.

Peter Smith is on the fund's steering committee. A retired math professor from South Bend, Indiana, where he runs the St. Augustine Soup Kitchen, he has an infectious, elfin smile that bursts through a long white beard. You probably wouldn't guess from looking at him that he was once an ROTC student who pulled his opinions from the John Birch Society.

"I wasn't a gung-ho military person at any time," Smith explained, "but I also wasn't opposed. I grew up Catholic and I was involved with the Knights of Columbus who were really supportive of the Vietnam War. I didn't get anything in my background that would indicate to me that there was anything wrong with war, and I never thought about the death and destruction that it caused."

From college, Smith embarked on a four-year Navy stint, assigned to a destroyer in the west Pacific. Afterwards, inspired by Martin Luther King's opposition to the Vietnam War and his arguments for Christian pacifism and nonviolent resistance, Smith turned his back on the military. He began to counsel men on how to avoid the draft and, in 1969, he started refusing to pay part of his federal income taxes.

He has been refusing ever since. "I don't keep the money," Smith said. "I send it to organizations that I know are going to be helping people. I end up paying the whole tax, but I don't pay it to the government."

Smith doesn't understand why more antiwar activists don't join him. "It just seems so obvious ... if you're against war you shouldn't pay for it. The IRS is kind of a scary institution and I guess people feel like they don't want to mess with it."

Many people think if you refuse to pay taxes you'll end up behind bars, but this is actually very rare. Of the tens of thousands of people who have resisted war taxes over the past 75 years, the National War Tax Resistance Coordinating Committee, or NWTRCC, knows of only 30 who have done time.

Although Smith has refused to pay for over 40 years, he said he's never faced jail or criminal charges because of it. "The IRS would just as soon collect the money and sock you with fines and interest," he said.

That's where the Penalty Fund comes in. It fully reimburses resisters for penalties and interest, thereby taking the sting out of IRS reprisals.

The IRS often fails to collect penalties, interest, or anything at all from determined resisters. Some resisters live lives of voluntary simplicity and have nothing for the IRS to seize (or owe no income tax in the first place). Others hide their assets. And sometimes the IRS drops the ball and lets the statute of limitations expire without attempting to collect. An informal poll at a national gathering of resisters in 2011 found that the IRS had taken only about a quarter of the hundreds of thousands of dollars those resisters had refused to pay over the years.

But not everyone is so lucky. Smith says the IRS took just about everything they wanted from him—garnishing his salary and seizing money from his bank and retirement accounts: over $100,000 in all. If you're unlucky you're also on the hook for penalties (which can eventually climb to 25 percent of what you refuse to pay) and interest. For example, if you refused to pay $6,000 in federal income tax when you filed your return in 2014, by the following April, at the interest rates operative at that time, the IRS would have added another $600, and the amount would continue to climb from there. Smith said "many folks find that the penalties and interest sometimes accumulate almost as much as the original principal that the IRS said they owed."

Shulamith Eagle, a war tax resister from Middlebury, Vermont, who is on the fund's steering committee, says that support from people who believe in her stand strengthens her resolve in the face of these IRS reprisals. "Some of us can't afford the financial penalties of tax refusal," she said. "With the penalty fund, we can afford this type of protest because we'll end up paying only the actual tax owed."

Eagle says the fund reminds her of the South African tradition of stokvel—or small mutual savings and investment programs — held by Christian congregations that organize mutual aid health insurance, and also of more spontaneous generosity. "Look at what happens when there is a weather or illness tragedy and it's publicized—money pours in from everywhere," she said. "Human beings are very generous people, and are willing to sacrifice where ethical protest is involved."

When people tell Smith that they admire his stand and wish they had the courage to do it, he tells them to subscribe to the fund. That way they can help other resisters until they work up the courage to do it themselves. "You don't have to be a war tax resister to support people," he said. "Anybody who wants to can sign up to help, and it's easy to do."

A survey of fund contributors found that many were not tax resisters. "Some people, because of family responsibilities or other reasons, can't [resist]," Eagle said. "This way they can participate indirectly. It's a blessing to help other people work to change things that must be changed, whether directly or indirectly. People said this over and over in their answers to the survey."

And it's a legal way to help people who are willing to risk civil disobedience, according to Peter Goldberger, an attorney who specializes in war tax resistance cases. "The penalty fund runs as a sort of insurance plan," he said. "I can't think of any way it would be illegal—either a violation of tax law or of criminal law —to plan to mitigate the consequences of other folks' getting into trouble for their own choices. There have long been 'bail funds' that crowd-source getting poor people or arrested demonstrators out of jail, for example, and folks that pay the criminal fines of others who are arrested for civil disobedience that the funders support in principle."

The fund has about 220 subscribers and it issues appeals a couple of times a year, asking subscribers to contribute about

$30 apiece. Each person who applies for reimbursement provides IRS transcripts—showing the amount that was collected and how much came from interest and penalties—and also some evidence that they resisted taxes because of their conscientious objection to war.

"As of now we have been able to pretty much reimburse everybody for what they have asked for," Smith said. The fund struggles more to find resisters to reimburse than to find money. Smith stresses that you don't have to be a subscriber to apply for reimbursement: you just have to be a war tax resister who has lost interest and penalties to the IRS.

Encouraging resisters to ask for reimbursements is one challenge the fund faces. Recruiting subscribers is another. "We use word of mouth and tabling at NWTRCC meetings and other conferences," Smith said. There's also some drudgery involved: Someone has to maintain the database of subscribers. Sending appeals—a process that still relies mostly on snail-mail—is time-consuming. But their hard work means the government has to work harder to discourage war tax resisters. Hitting a few resisters with fines and penalties will not be enough to scare them off.

14

Resisting War Tax Is as Necessary Today as It Was in Colonial America

War Resisters League

The War Resisters League was formed in New York City in 1923 by teacher Jessie Wallace Hughan as a successor to the prior Anti-Enlistment League, which had opposed US enlistment during World War I. It is the oldest secular pacifist organization in the United States and actively organized against the wars in Iraq and Afghanistan.

In this viewpoint written by members of the War Resisters League, the history of the modern war tax resistance movement is examined. As seen in the league's history, war tax resistance has been used in the United States from colonial America until the present day, with increased organizing during the world wars. An update of the article includes the call for war tax resisters to step up once again during the Donald Trump presidency in the face of increased military spending and renewed interest in peace and justice activism.

Refusing to pay taxes for war is probably as old as the first taxes levied for warfare.

Up until World War II, war tax resistance in the U.S. primarily manifested itself among members of the historic peace churches —Quakers, Mennonites, and Brethren—and usually only during times of war. There have been instances of people refusing to pay taxes for war in virtually every American war, but it was not until

"History of War Tax Resistance," War Resisters League, warresisters.org. Reprinted by permission.

World War II and the establishment of a permanent, centralized U.S. military (symbolized by the building of the Pentagon) was the modern war tax resistance movement born.

Colonial America

One of the earliest known instances of war tax refusal took place in 1637 when the relatively peaceable Algonquin Indians opposed taxation by the Dutch to help improve a local Dutch fort. Shortly after the Quakers arrived in America (1656) there were a number of individual instances of war tax resistance. In 1709 the Quaker Assembly refused a request of £4000 for an expedition into Canada, replying "it was contrary to their religious principles to hire men to kill one another."

American Revolution

Most Quakers were opposed to taxes designated specifically for military purposes. Though the official position of the Society of Friends was against any payment of war taxes. Property was seized and auctioned, and many Quakers were jailed for their war tax resistance. A number of Quakers even refused the "mixed taxes." Up to 500 Quakers were disowned for paying war taxes or joining the army.

Following the war many Quakers continued to refuse because these taxes were being used to pay the war debt, and therefore were essentially war taxes.

Mexican War

The Quakers reacted strongly to this war because of its aggressive nature and the threatened spread of slavery posed by the war. Many, again, refused to pay war taxes. However, the most famous instance of war tax resistance was that of Henry David Thoreau. Although not a pacifist he was opposed to slavery, and the imperialist and unjust nature of the war. His refusal to pay the Massachusetts poll tax levied for the war resulted in a night in jail. This whole experience was recorded in his essay, "On the Duty of Civil Disobedience," which has had a profound influence on many people since.

World War II

Until World War II the individual income tax was a minor part of the federal government receipts (affecting no more than 3 percent of the population). However with the introduction of the employee withholding tax in 1943, for the first time a large percentage of the population was subject to the income tax. The unprecedented amount of money being raised and spent for World War II suddenly touched the consciousness of many pacifists, who up until the war were not required to pay taxes.

In 1942 Ernest Bromley refused payment of $7.09 for a "defense tax stamp" required for all cars, and thus became the first known war tax resister in the modern era. He was arrested and eventually jailed for 60 days. Though Bromley and a few other pacifists did not pay income taxes during World War II, but there was no movement of war tax refusal.

Post-World War II

In April of 1948 a conference on "More Disciplined and Revolutionary Pacifist Activity" was held in Chicago, attended by over 300 people. The Call to the Conference (signed by A.J. Muste, Dave Dellinger, Harrop Freeman, George Houser, Dwight Macdonald, Ernest Bromley, and Marion Bromley, among others) expressed a need for a more revolutionary pacifist program and action techniques. Out of this conference grew a new organization, calling itself the Peacemakers. Their newsletter was titled Peacemaker. About forty people who attended the conference stated their intention to refuse part or all of their federal income taxes, forming a Tax Refusal Committee.

This Committee began almost immediately to publish news bulletins, independent of the Peacemaker. The bulletins were instrumental in engendering concern and giving information on tax refusal. War tax refusal succeeded in achieving nationwide publicity in 1949 with the issue of a Peacemaker press release titled "Forty-one Refuse to Pay Income Tax." For almost twenty years Peacemakers was virtually the only consistent source of information and support for war tax resisters. The Catholic Worker, The Progressive, Fellowship, and a few other movement newsletters and magazines, would occasionally print sympathetic articles on war tax resistance.

Following World War II and up to the start of the Vietnam War only six people were imprisoned for war tax resistance related issues: James Otsuka, Maurice McCrackin, Juanita Nelson, Eroseanna Robinson, Walter Gormly, and Arthur Evans. All had been found in contempt of court for refusing to cooperate in one way or another with the proceedings.

In 1963 the Peacemakers published the first handbook on war tax resistance, appropriately titled Handbook on Nonpayment of War Taxes.

Indochina War

War tax resistance gained nationwide publicity when Joan Baez announced in 1964 her refusal to pay 60 percent of her 1963 income taxes because of the war in Vietnam. In 1965 the Peacemakers formed the "No Tax for War in Vietnam Committee," obtaining signers to the pledge "I am not going to pay taxes on 1964 income." By 1967 about 500 people had signed the pledge.

Then several events in the mid- to late-1960s occurred making this a pivotal period for the war resistance movement, signaling a shift in war tax resistance from a couple hundred to eventually tens of thousands of refusers.

A committee led by A.J. Muste obtained 370 signatures (including Joan Baez, Lawrence Ferlinghetti, David Dellinger, Dorothy Day, Noam Chomsky, Nobel Prize winner Albert Szent-Gyorgyi, publisher Lyle Stuart, and Staughton Lynd) for an ad in The Washington Post, which proclaimed their intention not to pay all or part of their 1965 income taxes.

A suggestion in 1966 to form a mass movement around the refusal to pay the (at that time) 10 percent telephone tax was given an initial boost by Chicago tax resister Karl Meyer. This was followed by War Resisters League developing a national campaign in the late 1960s to encourage refusal to pay the telephone tax.

In 1967, Gerald Walker of *The New York Times Magazine* began the organizing of Writers and Editors War Tax Protest. The 528 writers and editors (including Gloria Steinem and Kirkpatrick Sale) pledged themselves to refuse the 10 percent war surtax (which had just been added to income taxes) and possibly the 23 percent of their income tax allocated for the war. Most daily newspapers refused to sell space for the ad. Only the New York Post (at that time, a liberal newspaper), Ramparts (a popular left-wing anti-war magazine), and the New York Review of Books carried it. To see an image of the ad, click on link above.

Ken Knudson, in a 1965 letter to the Peacemaker, suggested that inflating the W-4 form would stop withholding. Again, Karl Meyer was instrumental in promoting this idea, which was adopted by Peacemakers, Catholic Worker, and War Resisters League, among other organizations in the late 1960s. Inflating W-4 forms also brought a new wave of indictments and jailings by the government —16 were indicted for claiming too many dependents; of those, six were actually jailed.

The number of known income tax resisters grew from 275 in 1966 to an estimated 20,000 in the early 1970s. The number of telephone tax resisters was estimated to be in the hundreds of thousands. Many groups were formed around the country including "people's life funds," to which people sent their war tax resisted money to fund community programs.

The popularity of war tax resistance grew to such an extent that the WRL could no longer handle the volume of requests. So in 1969 a press conference was held in New York City to announce the founding of the National War Tax Resistance (WTR). Long-time peace activist Bradford Lyttle was the first coordinator. Local WTR chapters blossomed around the country, and by 1972 there were 192 such groups. WTR published a comprehensive handbook on tax resistance, Ain't Gonna Pay for War No More (edited by Robert Calvert), and put out a monthly newsletter, Tax Talk. Radical members of the historic peace churches began to urge their constituencies to refuse war taxes.

In 1972 Congressman Ronald Dellums (CA) introduced the World Peace Tax Fund Act in Congress, which was designed to create a conscientious objector status for taxpayers. The National Council for a World Peace Tax Fund was formed to promote this legislation (later changed to National Campaign for a Peace Tax Fund). The bill has been introduced into each Congress since.

During the Indochina War, war tax resistance gained its greatest strength ever in the history of the United States, and on a secular basis rather than as a result of the historic peace churches, who played a very minor role this time. The government did its best to stop this increase in tax resistance, but was hamstrung by telephone tax resisters. There were so many resisters and so little tax owed per person that the IRS lost money every time they made a collection. The cost of bank levies, garnished wages, automobile and property seizures, and even the simplest IRS paperwork was simply too expensive to be worth it.

The Reagan Military Escalation

National WTR folded in 1975 with the end of the Indochina War. By 1977 war tax resistance dropped to about 20,000 telephone tax resisters and a few thousand income tax resisters. Then in 1978 some radical members of the three historic peace churches got together to issue a "New Call to Peacemaking" that suggested war tax resistance as one way to oppose the arms race. The Center on Law and Pacifism was formed in 1978 to assist these and other war tax resistance efforts, issuing the book People Pay for Peace (by William Durland) in 1979.

With the election of Ronald Reagan as President in 1980 and his call to rearm the U.S., many more people began to resist war taxes. The IRS admitted the number of war tax resisters tripled between 1978 and 1981. Like Joan Baez's tax refusal announcement seventeen years before, a national stir was created in 1981 when Roman Catholic Archbishop Raymond Hunthausen of Seattle urged citizens to refuse to pay 50 percent of their income taxes to protest spending on nuclear weapons. Letters of endorsement of his stand were made by other religious leaders in Seattle and elsewhere around the country.

In 1982 the War Resisters League published the first edition of The Guide to War Tax Resistance, which sought to provide a broad and comprehensive source of information incorporating the out-of-print Ain't Gonna Pay for War No More, Peacemakers' Handbook on the Nonpayment of War Taxes, as well as new material not included in either book. A fifth edition of the book came out in 2003. About the same time, WRL began producing its annual "tax piechart" street flyer, which analyzed the spending of the Federal government while promoting protests to military spending.

This renewed interest in war tax resistance, spurred on by the unprecedented increase in military spending during peacetime, stimulated an escalated response by the government. Though there have been only three criminal prosecutions of war tax resisters since 1980, the IRS shifted tactics and began seizing property. In 1984 and 1985 after almost ten years of very few seizures, about a half dozen automobiles and a similar number of houses were seized from war tax resisters. Furthermore, in 1982 the government came up with a new civil penalty which was specifically aimed at war tax resisters. Called the "frivolous" fine, it charged a $500 penalty against anyone who altered their 1040 forms (e.g., by claiming a war tax deduction).

In an effort to coordinate the growing interest in war tax resistance, a National Action Conference was called by WRL and the Center on Law and Pacifism in 1982. Out of this conference the National War Tax Resistance Coordinating Committee (NWTRCC) was formed. Every spring NWTRCC has issued press releases announcing Tax Day actions around the country. In addition to a bimonthly newsletter with the latest war tax resistance news,

NWTRCC has issued several brochures, produced a slide show, and published the War Tax Manual for Counselors and Lawyers.

The End of the "Cold War"

In 1989 with the fall of the Berlin Wall, followed by the collapse of the former Soviet bloc, and the dissolution of the Soviet Union, the Cold War ended. War tax resisters and others expected a major reduction in the U.S. military and looked for ways to work in coalition with groups calling for a "peace dividend." However, a little more than a year later, George Bush sent U.S. troops to the Persian Gulf region, and war tax resistance groups were flooded with calls from people saying that they'd "had enough!"

Also in 1989, the IRS seized and auctioned the Colrain, MA, home of war tax resisters Randy Kehler and Betsy Corner; shortly thereafter, the home of resisters Bob Bady and Pat Morse, neighbors of Kehler-Corner, was also seized and auctioned. Within hours, a support committee was formed. Significant articles appeared in newspapers across the country. After their eviction in 1991, the house was occupied by a rotating collection of affinity groups until 1992, when the new owners forced their way in. A continuous vigil outside lasted until the fall of 1993. Throughout this entire period, considerable publicity, actions, and support were generated bringing a lot of attention to war tax resistance, U.S. military spending, and the misplaced priorities of the government. Four years later "An Act of Conscience," a 90-minute film about the struggle, was finished.

Meanwhile, from 1990 to 1993 the Alternative Revenue Service (ARS) was developed by the WRL and co-sponsored by NWTRCC and the Conscience and Military Tax Campaign. It grew out of a desire, shared by many war tax resisters, to have a nationally organized campaign that would reach out to new communities in a creative way, suggesting that even a token level of tax resistance is a valuable protest. During the 1990-1991 tax season, 70,000 EZ Peace forms—a parody of the IRS's 1040EZ form—were circulated.

About 500 forms were returned and over $105,000 in resisted taxes were redirected to alternative funds and other groups. By 1993, a decline in interest, made that the last season for the ARS.

Numerous well-publicized cases of IRS abuse led to Congressional hearings in 1997 and 1998, and resulted in the IRS Restructuring and Reform Act. Among the changes, were some reductions in interest and penalties, some restrictions on levies and seizures, reorganizing the IRS away from a geographical structure to one that concentrates on types of taxpayers (individuals, small businesses and the self-employed, corporations, and tax-exempt groups), and a number of more cosmetic (as far as war tax resisters are concerned) changes. The IRS also cut back on the number of collection agents, liens, levies, and seizures of property.

In 1993 Congress passed the Religious Freedom Restoration Act in an attempt to accommodate individual conscience in instances where a person's religious beliefs may be adversely affected by the government. In the late 1990s three court cases were filed by Quaker war tax resisters using RFRA and the First Amendment guarantee to the free exercise of religion in an attempt to have penalties against war tax resisters removed and permit them to pay only for non-military programs. These cases were dismissed in lower courts, appealed, then dismissed again in the Second and Third Circuit Courts. In 2000 the U.S. Supreme Court declined to hear any of the appeals.

The "War on Terrorism" (2001-?)

Following the September 11, 2001, terrorist attacks on the World Trade Center and the Pentagon, President George W. Bush began bombing Afghanistan and sent in ground troops to topple the ruling Taliban regime in the name of fighting terrorism. In March 2003, the U.S. launched an all-out war against Iraq, a country with no role in the September 11 attacks. More than 15 years after the U.S. attack on Afghanistan, random bombings, drone strikes, and factional killings have spread to Pakistan, Syria, Yemen, Libya, and Somalia. Since 2001, the wars have cost more than $4 trillion, killed 1-2 million civilians, and created millions of refugees fleeing the violence.

War tax resisters acted in coalition with millions of others around the world to stop the invasion of Iraq and have continued to campaign against war spending ever since. In 2003 one of the largest public acts of war tax resistance and redirection occurred when environmental activist Julia Butterfly Hill announced her refusal to pay $100,000 in federal income taxes from a legal settlement because of the Iraq war. The Iraq Pledge of Resistance initiated an internet-based telephone tax resistance campaign, Hang Up On War, that was endorsed by a coalition of groups. Resisters developed an alternative tax form—a "Peace Tax Return"—to simplify resistance.

In July 2007 the Associated Press (AP) ran an article, "Fed Up With War, Some Won't Pay Taxes" by John Christoffersen that brought sig¬nificant attention to war tax resistance. The group Code Pink launched an online tax resistance pledge called "Don't Buy Bush's War," and National War Tax Resistance Coordinating Committee started the War Tax Boycott campaign and collected pledges of over $400,000 of redirected tax money to donate to organizations helping victims of war.

About six war tax resisters were jailed between 2006 and 2010 (but none to date since then), and the IRS continues to pressure individuals to pay or seizes money from bank accounts and salaries. With the ongoing wars and the increased militarism in the U.S., the peace movement and war tax resistance should have grown, but during the Obama presidency peace activism slipped into the background. In 2010 the National War Tax Resistance Coordinating Committee produced a half-hour video, Death and Taxes, about war tax resistance, which featured interviews with 28 people explaining why they resist.

The Occupy movement brought attention to income inequality, and war tax resisters were active in that movement. More recently, climate change and Black Lives Matter have moved to the forefront of activism in the U.S., but longtime peace movement groups carry on their work and war tax resistance has maintained a steady if not growing network.

In late 2016, facing the incoming administration of Donald Trump, activism for justice and peace is on the increase again, and war tax resistance is getting a new look from many people.

15

Online Activists Can Be Treated as Criminals Under the Computer Fraud and Abuse Act

Christie Thompson

Christie Thompson studied journalism at Northwestern University and is a former journalism intern at Propublica. She has written for the Nation, *the* Chicago Reporter, *and the* Atlantic.

As Christie Thompson shows in this viewpoint, the cyber world is a unique space where civil disobedience can play out. Departing from the well-known case of Aaron Swartz, the Reddit cofounder and internet activist who committed suicide in 2013 when he was accused of stealing and posting academic articles, Thompson examines the federal Computer Fraud and Abuse Act (CFAA), an act that was designed to fight against hackers. However, as Thompson shows, the CFAA is also useful to fight against those who commit acts of civil disobedience online, who can face, like Swartz, multiple felony counts, millions of dollars in fines, and as much as fifty years in prison. This is an issue that will continue to be explored in courts and among the public in years to come.

W hen Reddit co-founder and internet freedom activist Aaron Swartz committed suicide last Friday, he was facing up to 13 felony counts, 50 years in prison, and millions of dollars in fines.

"Hacktivism: Civil Disobedience or Cyber Crime?" by Christie Thompson, ProPublica, January 18, 2013. Reprinted by permission.

His alleged crime? Pulling millions of academic articles from the digital archive JSTOR.

Prosecutors allege that Swartz downloaded the articles because he intended to distribute them for free online, though Swartz was arrested before any articles were made public. He had often spoken publicly about the importance of making academic research freely available.

Other online activists have increasingly turned to computer networks and other technology as a means of political protest, deploying a range of tactics—from temporarily shutting down servers to disclosing personal and corporate information.

Most of these acts, including Swartz's downloads, are criminalized under the federal Computer Fraud and Abuse Act (CFAA), an act was designed to prosecute hackers. But as Swartz's and other "hacktivist" cases demonstrate, you don't necessarily have to be a hacker to be viewed as one under federal law. Are activists like Swartz committing civil disobedience, or online crimes? We break down a few strategies of "hacktivism" to see what is considered criminal under the CFAA.

Publishing Documents

Accessing and downloading documents from private servers or behind paywalls with the intent of making them publicly available.

Swartz gained access to JSTOR through MIT's network and downloaded millions of files, in violation of JSTOR's terms of service (though JSTOR declined to prosecute the case). Swartz had not released any of the downloaded files at the time his legal troubles began.

The most famous case of publishing private documents online may be the ongoing trial of Bradley Manning. While working as an intelligence analyst in Iraq, Manning passed thousands of classified intelligence reports and diplomatic cables to Wikileaks, to be posted on their website.

"I want people to see the truth... regardless of who they are... because without information, you cannot make informed decisions as a public," Manning wrote in an online chat with ex-hacker Adrian Lamo, who eventually turned Manning in to the Department of Defense.

Both Swartz and Manning were charged under a section of the CFAA that covers anyone who "knowingly causes the transmission of a program, information, code, or command, and as a result of such conduct, intentionally causes damage without authorization, to a protected computer..."

The charges hinge on an interpretation of this section that says anyone in violation of a website's terms of service is an unauthorized user. Because they're unauthorized, all of their activity on that website could therefore be considered illegal. Both were charged with felonies under the CFAA, on top of other allegations.

The Ninth and Fourth Circuit Court of Appeals have ruled that such an interpretation of the CFAA casts too wide a net. With the circuit courts divided over whether a broad definition of "unauthorized" is constitutional, it may fall on the Supreme Court to ultimately decide.

Assistant U.S. Attorney Steve Heymann of Massachusetts was the lead prosecutor in Swartz's case. (He was known for winning a 2010 case that landed hacker Albert Gonzalez 20 years in prison.) Heymann offered Swartz a plea bargain of six months in prison but Swartz's defense team rejected the deal, saying a felony and any time behind bars was too harsh a sentence. Swartz's family blamed his death in part on "intimidation and prosecutorial overreach."

As a result of Swartz's suicide, some lawmakers are now calling for a review of the CFAA. On Tuesday, Rep. Zoe Lofgren (D-Calif.) proposed a piece of legislation called "Aaron's Law," which would amend the law to explicitly state that merely violating a site's terms of service cannot fall under the federal CFAA.

Distributed Denial of Service

A Distributed Denial of Service, or DDoS attack, floods a web site's server with traffic from a network of sometimes thousands of individual computers, making it incapable of serving legitimate traffic.

In 2010, the group Anonymous attempted to overload websites for PayPal, Visa and Mastercard after the companies refused to process donations to Wikileaks. Anonymous posted their "Low Orbit Ion Canon" software online, allowing roughly 6,000 people who downloaded the program to pummel the sites with traffic.

A DDoS attack can be charged as a crime under the CFAA, as it "causes damage" and can violate a web site's terms of service. The owner of the site could also file a civil suit citing the CFAA, if they can prove a temporary server overload resulted in monetary losses.

Sixteen alleged members of Anonymous were arrested for their role in the PayPal DDoS, and could face more than 10 years in prison and $250,000 in fines. They were charged with conspiracy and "intentional damage to a protected computer" under the CFAA and the case is ongoing.

Some web activists have pressed for DDoS to be legalized as a form of protest, claiming that disrupting web traffic by occupying a server is the same as clogging streets when staging a sit-in. A petitionstarted on the White House's "We the People" site a few days before Swartz's death has garnered more than 5,000 signatures.

"Distributed denial-of-service (DDoS) is not any form of hacking in any way," the petition reads. "It is the equivalent of repeatedly hitting the refresh button on a webpage. It is, in that way, no different than any 'occupy' protest."

Doxing

Doxing involves finding and publishing a target's personal or corporate information.

In 2011, Anonymous and hacker group Lulzsec breached the Stratfor Global Intelligence Service database and published the passwords, addresses and credit card information of the firm's high-profile clients. The group claimed they planned to use the credit cards to donate $1 million to charity.

Anonymous also recently doxed members of the Westboro Baptist Church after several tweeted their plans to picket funerals for Sandy Hook victims. Hackers were able to access Church members' twitter accounts and publish their personal information, including phone numbers, emails and hotel reservation details.

Jeremy Hammond could face life in prison for allegedly leading the Stratfor hack and a separate attack on the Arizona Department of Safety website. Former Anonymous spokesman Barrett Brown was also indicted for computer fraud in the Stratfor dox, not for hacking into the system, but for linking to the hacked information in a chat room.

The charges for doxing depend on how the information was accessed, and the nature of published information. Simply publishing publicly available information, such as phone numbers found in a Google search, would probably not be charged under the CFAA. But hacking into private computers, or even spreading the information from a hack, could lead to charges under the CFAA.

16

Hacktivism Will Become an Important Tool in Future Civil Disobedience

Gavin Mueller

Gavin Mueller holds a PhD in cultural studies from George Mason University. He is a visiting assistant professor of emerging media and communication at the University of Texas at Dallas.

In this review for Molly Sauter's The Coming Swarm, *Gavin Mueller examines how civil disobedience has changed in the age of cyber warfare. Steeped in academic jargon and theory, this viewpoint nevertheless argues very basically that the "hacktivist" technique called distributed denial of service (DDoS) can be used as political action against unjust corporate interests online. DDoS is a technique in which online activists working together can disrupt service to specific websites and internet servers. However, as examined in the previous article, this is a new form of civil disobedience that must be experimented with as we discover the ways in which it can and cannot be viably used against injustice.*

Molly Sauter's *The Coming Swarm* begins in an odd way. Ethan Zuckerman, director of MIT's Center for Civic Media, confesses in the book's foreword that he disagrees with the book's central argument: that distributed denial of service (DDoS) actions, where specific websites and/or internet servers are overwhelmed

"Civil Disobedience in the Age of Cyberwar," by Gavin Mueller, boundary2.org, July 13, 2016. https://www.boundary2.org/2016/07/civil-disobedience-in-the-age-of-cyberwar/. Licensed under CC BY 4.0 International.

by traffic and knocked offline via the coordinated activity of many computers acting together, should be viewed as a legitimate means of protest.[1] "My research demonstrated that these attacks, once mounted by online extortionists as a form of digital protection racket, were increasingly being mounted by governments as a way of silencing critics," Zuckerman writes (xii). Sauter's argument, which takes the form of this slim and knotty book, ultimately does not convince Zuckerman, though he admits he is "a better scholar and a better person" for having engaged with the arguments contained within. "We value civic arguments, whether they unfold in the halls of government, a protest encampment, or the comments thread of an internet post because we believe in the power of deliberation" (xv). This promise of the liberal public sphere is what Sauter grapples with throughout the work, to varying levels of success.

The Coming Swarm is not a book about DDoS activities in general. As Sauter notes, "DDoS is a popular tactic of extortion, harassment, and silencing" (6): its most common uses come from criminal organizations and government cyberwar operations. Sauter is not interested in these kinds of actions, which encompass the vast majority of DDoS uses. (DDoS itself is a subset of all denial of service or DoS attacks.) Instead they focus on self-consciously political DDoS attacks, first carried out by artist-hacker groups in the 1990s (the electrohippies and the Electronic Disturbance Theater) and more recent actions by the group Anonymous.[2] All told, these are a handful of actions, barely numbering in the double digits, and spread out over two decades. The focus on this small minority of cases can make the book's argument seem question-begging, since Sauter does not make clear how and why it is legitimate to analyze exclusively those few instances of a widespread phenomenon that happen to conform to an author's desired outlook. At one level, this is a general problem throughout the book, since Sauter's analysis is confined to what they call "activist DDoS," yet the actual meaning of this term is rarely interrogated: viewed from the perspective of the actors, many of the DDoS actions Sauter dismisses by stipulation could also be–and likely are–viewed as "activism."

From its earliest inception, political DDoS actions were likened to "virtual sit-ins": activists use their computers' ability to ping a server to clog up its functioning, potentially slowing or bringing its activity to a stand-still. This situated the technique within a history of nonviolent civil disobedience, particularly that of the Civil Rights Movement. This metaphor has tended to overdetermine the debate over the use of DDoS in activist contexts, and Sauter is keen to move on from the connection: "such comparisons on the part of the media and the public serve to only stifle innovation within social movements and political action, while at the same time cultivating a deep and unproductive nostalgia for a kind of 'ideal activism' that never existed" (22-3). Sauter argues that not only does this leave out contributions to the Civil Rights Movement that the mainstream finds less than respectable; it helps rule out the use of disruptive and destructive forms of activism in future movements.

This argument has merit, and many activists who want to move beyond nonviolent civil disobedience into direct action forms of political action appear to agree with it. Yet Sauter still wants to claim the label of civil disobedience for DDoS actions that they at other moments discard: "activist DDoS actions are not meaningfully different from other actions within the history of civil disobedience... novelty cannot properly exempt activist DDoS from being classified as a tactic of civil disobedience" (27). However, the main criticisms of DDoS as civil disobedience have nothing to do with its novelty. As Evgeny Morozov points out in his defense of DDoS as a political tactic, "I'd argue, however, that the DDoS attacks launched by Anonymous were not acts of civil disobedience because they failed one crucial test implicit in Rawls's account: Most attackers were not willing to accept the legal consequences of their actions." Novelist and digital celebrity Cory Doctorow, who opposes DDoS-based activism, echoes this concern: "A sit-in derives its efficacy not from merely blocking the door to some objectionable place, but from the public willingness to stand before your neighbours and risk arrest and bodily harm in service of a moral cause, which is itself a force for moral suasion." The complaint is not that DDoS fails to live up to the standards of the Civil Rights Movement, or that it is too novel. It is that it often fails the basic test of civil disobedience: potentially subjecting oneself to punishment as a form of protest that lays bare the workings of the state.

Zuckerman's principle critique of Sauter's arguments is that DDoS, by shutting down sites, censors speech opposed by activists rather than promoting their dissenting messages. Sauter has a two-pronged response to this. First, they say that DDoS attacks make the important point that the internet is not really a public space. Instead, it is controlled by private interests, with large corporations managing the vast majority of online space. This means that no arguments may rest, implicitly or explicitly, on the assumption that the internet is a Habermasian public sphere. Second, Sauter argues, by their own admission counterintuitively, that DDoS, properly contextualized as part of "communicative capitalism," is itself a form of speech.

Communicative capitalism is a term developed by Jodi Dean as part of her critique of the Habermasian vision of the internet as a public sphere. With the commodification of online speech, "the exchange value of messages overtakes their use value" (58). The communication of messages is overwhelmed by the priority to circulate content of any kind: "communicative exchanges, rather than being fundamental to democratic politics, are the basic elements of capitalist production" (56). For Dean, this logic undermines political effects from internet communication: "The proliferation, distribution, acceleration and intensification of communicative access and opportunity, far from enhancing democratic governance or resistance, results in precisely the opposite—the post-political formation of communicative capitalism" (53). If, Sauter argues, circulation itself becomes the object of communication, the power of DDoS is to disrupt that circulation of context. "In that context the interruption of that signal becomes an equally powerful contribution.... Under communicative capitalism, it is possible that it is the intentional creation of disruptions and silence that is the most powerful contribution" (29).

However, this move is contrary to the point of Dean's concept; Dean specifically rejects the idea that any kind of communicative activity puts forth real political antagonism. Dean's argument is, admittedly, an overreach. While capital cares little for the specificity of messages, human beings do: as Marx notes, exchange value cannot exist without a use value. Sauter's own "counterintuitive" use of Dean points to a larger difficulty with Sauter's argument: it remains wedded to a liberal understanding of political action grounded in the idea of a public sphere. Even when Sauter moves on to discussing DDoS as disruptive direct action, rather than civil disobedience, they return to the discursive tropes of the public sphere: DDoS is "an attempt to assert a fundamental view of the internet as a 'public forum' in the face of its attempted designation as 'private property'" (45). Direct action is evaluated by its contribution to "public debate," and Sauter even argues that DDoS actions during the 1999 Seattle WTO protests did not infringe on the "rights" of delegates to attend the event because they were totally ineffective. This overlooks the undemocratic and illiberal character of the WTO itself, whose meetings were held behind closed doors (one of the major rhetorical points of the protest), and it implies that the varieties of direct action that successfully blockaded meetings could be morally compromised. These kinds of actions, bereft of an easy classification as forms of speech or communication, are the forms of antagonistic political action Dean argues cannot be found in online space.

In this light, it is worth returning to some of the earlier theorizations of DDoS actions. The earliest DDoS activists the electrohippies and Electronic Disturbance Theater documented the philosophies behind their work, and Rita Raley's remarkable book Tactical Media presented a bracing theoretical synthesis of DDoS as an emergent critical art-activist practice. EDT's most famous action deployed its FloodNet DDoS tool in pro-Zapatista protests.

Its novel design incorporated something akin to speech acts: for example, it pinged servers belonging to the Mexican government with requests for "human rights," leading to a return message "human rights not found on this server," a kind of technopolitical pun. Yet Raley rejects a theorization of online political interventions strictly in terms of their communicative value. Rather they are a curious hybrid of artistic experiment and militant interrogation, a Deleuzian event where one endeavors "to act without knowing the situation into which one will be propelled, to change things as they exist" (26).

The goal of EDT's actions was not simply to have a message be heard, or even to garner media attention: as EDT's umbrella organization the Critical Art Ensemble puts it in Electronic Civil Disobedience, "The indirect approach of media manipulation using a spectacle of disobedience designed to muster public sympathy and support is a losing proposition" (15). Instead, EDT took on the prerogatives of conceptual art—to use creative practice to pose questions and provoke response—in order to probe the contours of the emerging digital terrain and determine who would control it and how. That their experiments quickly raised the specter of terrorism, even in a pre-9/11 context, seemed to answer this. As Raley describes, drawing from RAND cyberwar researchers, DDoS and related tactics "shift the Internet 'from the public sphere model and casts it more as conflicted territory bordering on a war zone.'" (44).

While Sauter repeatedly criticizes treating DDoS actions as criminal, rather than political, acts, the EDT saw its work as both, and even analogous to terrorism. "Not that the activists are initiating terrorist practice, since no one dies in hyperreality, but the effect of this practice can have the same consequence as terrorism, in that state and corporate power vectors will haphazardly return fire with weapons that have destructive material (and even mortal) consequences" (25). Indeed, civil disobedience is premised on exploiting the ambiguities of activities that can be considered both crime and politics. Rather than attempt to fix distinctions after the fact, EDT recognized the power of such actions precisely in collapsing these distinctions. EDT did criticize the overcriminalization of online activity, as does Sauter, whose analysis of the use of the Computer Fraud and Abuse Act to prosecute DDoS activities is some of the book's strongest and most useful material.

Sauter prefers the activities of Anonymous to the earlier actions by the electrohippies and EDT (although EDT co-founder Ricardo Dominguez has been up to his old tricks: he was investigated by the FBI and threatened with revocation of tenure for a "virtual sit-in" against the University of California system during the student occupations of 2010). This is because Anonymous' actions, with their unpretentious lulzy ardor and open-source tools, "lower the barriers to entry" to activism (104): in other words, they leverage the internet's capacity to increase participation. For Sauter, the value in Anonymous' use of its DDoS tool, the Low Orbit Ion Cannon, against targets such as the MPAA and PayPal "lay in the media attention and new participants it attracted, who sympathized with Anonymous' views and could participate in future actions" (115). The benefit of collaborative open-source development is similar, as is the tool's feature that allows a user to contribute their computer to a "voluntary botnet" called the "[expletive] HIVE MIND" which "allows for the temporary sharing of an activist identity, which subsequently becomes more easily adopted by those participants who opt to remain involved" (130). This tip of the hat to theorists of participatory media once again reveals the notion of a democratic public sphere as a regulative ideal for the text.

The price of all this participation is that a "lower level of commitment was required" (129) from activists, which is oddly put forth as a benefit. In fact, Sauter criticizes FloodNet's instructions— "send your own message to the error log of the institution/symbol of Mexican Neo-Liberalism of your choice"—as relying upon "specialized language that creates a gulf between those who already understand it and those who do not" (112). Not only is it unclear to me what the specialized language in this case is ("neoliberalism" is a widely used, albeit not universally understood term), but it seems paramount that individuals opting to engage in risky political action should understand the causes for which they are putting themselves on the line. Expanding political participation is a laudable goal, but not at the expense of losing the content of politics. Furthermore, good activism requires training: several novice Anons were caught and prosecuted for participating in DDoS actions due to insufficient operational security measures.

What would it mean to take seriously the idea that the internet is not, in fact, a public sphere, and that, furthermore, the liberal notion of discursive and communicative activities impacting the decisions of rational individuals does not, in fact, adequately describe contemporary politics? Sauter ends up in a compelling place, one akin to the earlier theorists of DDoS: war. After all, states are one of the major participants in DDoS, and Sauter documents how Britain's Government Communications Headquarters (GCHQ) used Denial of Service attacks, even though deemed illegal, against Anonymous itself. The involvement of state actors "could portend the establishment of a semipermanent state of cyberwar" with activists rebranded as criminals and even terrorists. This is consonant with Raley's analysis of EDT's own forays into online space. It also recalls the radical political work of ultraleft formations such as Tiqqun (I had anticipated that The Coming Swarm was a reference to The Coming Insurrection though this does not seem to be the case), for whom war, specifically civil war, becomes the governing metaphor for antagonistic political practice under Empire.

This would mean that the future of DDoS actions and other disruptive online activism would not be in its mobilization of speech, but in its building of capacities and organization of larger politicized formations. This could potentially be an opportunity to consider the varieties of DDoS so often bracketed away, which often rely on botnets and operate in undeniably criminal ways. Current hacker formations use these practices in political ways (Ghost Squad has recently targeted the U.S. military, cable news stations, the KKK and Black Lives Matters among others with DDoS, accompanying each action with political manifestos). While Sauter claims, no doubt correctly, that these activities are "damaging to [DDoS's] perceived legitimacy as an activist tactic (160), they also note that measures to circumvent DDoS "continue to outstrip the capabilities of nearly all activist campaigns" (159). If DDoS has a future as a political tactic, it may be in the zones beyond what liberal political theory can touch.

Notes

[1] Instances of DDoS are typically referred to in both the popular press and by hacktivsts as "attacks." Sauter prefers the term "actions," a usage I follow here.

[2] I follow Sauter's preferred usage of the pronouns "they" and "them."

Works Cited

Critical Art Ensemble. 1996. *Electronic Civil Disobedience.* Brooklyn: Autonomedia.

Dean, Jodi. 2005. "Communicative Capitalism: Circulation and the Foreclosure of Politics." Cultural Politics 1.1. 51-74.

Raley, Rita. 2009. *Tactical Media.* Minneapolis: University of Minnesota Press.

Sauter, Molly. 2014. *The Coming Swarm: DDoS Actions, Hacktivism, and Civil Disobedience on the Internet.* New York: Bloomsbury Academic.

Organizations to Contact

The editors have compiled the following list of organizations concerned with the issues debated in this book. The descriptions are derived from materials provided by the organizations. All have publications or information available for interested readers. The list was compiled on the date of publication of the present volume; the information provided here may change. Be aware that many organizations take several weeks or longer to respond to inquiries, so allow as much time as possible.

ADAPT
1640-A E. 2nd Street, Suite 1000
Austin, Texas 78702
(512) 442-0252
email: adapt@adapt.org
website: www.adapt.org

ADAPT is a national grassroots organization that organizes its members to fight for disability rights through civil disobedience and non-violent action. ADAPT is a national organization with several local bureaus, including in Denver, Colorado.

American Civil Liberties Union (ACLU)
125 Broad Street, 18th Floor
New York, NY 10004
(212) 549-2500
email: membership@aclu.org
website: www.aclu.org

The ACLU is an activist organization that works in courts, legislatures, and communities around the United States to defend the liberties guaranteed in the US Constitution. It has been at the forefront of activism for civil liberties for the last one hundred years and often defends activists who have been arrested because of civil disobedience.

The American Friends Service Committee of Nonviolent Direct Action and Civil Disobedience (AFSC-NDACD)

1501 Cherry Street
Philadelphia, PA 191102
(215) 241-7000
email: https://www.afsc.org/contact
website: www.afsc.org

The AFSC is a Quaker organization dedicated to promoting peace throughout the world. Their organization is based on the belief that every person has worth and that the power of love can overcome violence and injustice. Quaker organizations such as the AFSC have long been at the forefront of civil disobedience in the face of unjust laws.

Code Pink

2010 Linden Avenue
Venice, CA 90291
(310) 827-4320
email: info@codepink.org
website: www.codepink.org

Code Pink is a women-led grassroots organization that began in 2002 in an effort to prevent the US war in Iraq. Today, Code Pink fights to end all unjust wars and militarism, to support human rights, and to increase access to health care, education, and green jobs for all. Code Pink uses local organizers and has successfully led many peaceful protests around the globe.

Democracy Spring

email: democracyspring@gmail.com
website: www.democracyspring.org

Democracy Spring is a political action organization dedicated to removing "big money" from politics and guaranteeing the right to vote. In April 2016, Democracy Spring organized the single largest action of civil disobedience in the United States in the twenty-first century when the organization brought 1,300 people to Washington, DC, to protest corruption in politics.

The National Association for the Advancement of Colored People (NAACP)
4805 Mt. Hope Drive
Baltimore, MD 21215
(410) 580-5777
email: washingtobureau@naacpnet.org
website: www.naacp.org

The NAACP was founded in 1909 and is the nation's oldest, largest, and most recognized civil rights organization. Today, it has over half a million members. The organization took a leading role during the civil rights movement and continues to support the rights of all people, regardless of their race, religion, or gender, in the United States and throughout the world.

Pax Christi USA (PCUSA)
415 Michigan Ave NE, Suite 240
Washington, DC 20017
(202) 635-2741
email: info@paxchristiusa.org
website: www.paxchristiusa.org

Pax Christi is an international Catholic organization, founded in 1945 in France that fights for peace. Begun in response to World War II and the holocaust in Europe, Pax Christi today uses civil disobedience to fight against war, any form of violence or domination, and racist practices.

The Sierra Club
2101 Webster Street, Suite 1300

Oakland, CA 94612
(415) 977-5500
email: information@sierraclub.org
website: www.sierraclub.org

Founded by the conservationist John Muir in 1892, The Sierra Club is the nation's largest environmental organization, with more than two million members. The organization works to protect the environment by setting aside public land for national parks and stopping the use of fossil fuels in the United States, among other goals. It has been vocal in its support of non-violent protest against the Dakota Access pipeline, as well as other pipeline projects.

The Thoreau Society
341 Virginia Road
Concord, MA 01742
(978) 369-5310
email: info@thoreausociety.org
website: www.thoreausociety.org

The Thoreau Society aims to advocate for Henry David Thoreau's legacy through outreach, education, and advocacy. It aims to teach American citizens the importance of living a "deliberate, considered" life, even if this involves actions of civil disobedience.

The War Resisters League (WRL)
168 Canal Street, Suite 600
New York, NY 10013
(212) 228-0450
email: wrl@warresisters.org
website: www.warresisters.org

Founded in 1923, the War Resisters League is the oldest secular pacifist organization in the United States. Its members work for nonviolent resolution to the world's political problems using a variety of civil disobedience techniques, including war tax resistance.

Bibliography

Books

Karen Armstrong. *Twelve Steps to a Compassionate Life*. New York, NY: Anchor, 2011.

Becky Bond and Zack Exley. *Rules for Revolutionaries: How Big Organizing Can Change Everything*. White River Junction, VT: Chelsea Green Publishing, 2016.

Angela Y. Davis. *Freedom is a Constant Struggle: Ferguson, Palestine, and the Foundations of a Movement*. Chicago, IL: Haymarket Books, 2016.

Mark Engler and Paul Engler. *This is an Uprising: How Nonviolent Revolt is Shaping the Twenty-First Century*. New York, NY: Nation Books, 2016.

Sarah Jaffe. *Necessary Trouble: Americans in Revolt*. Nation Books, 2016.

Greg Jobin-Leeds and AgitArte. When *We Fight, We Win: Twenty-First-Century Social Movements and the Activists That Are Transforming Our World*. The New Press, 2016.

John B. Judis. *The Populist Explosion: How the Great Recession Transformed American and European Politics*. New York, NY: Columbia Global Reports, 2016.

Mark Kurlandsky. *Nonviolence: The History of a Dangerous Idea*. New York, NY: Modern Library, 2008.

Doug McAdam. *Freedom Summer*. New York, NY: Oxford University Press, 1990.

Michael N. Nagler. *The Nonviolence Handbook: A Guide for Practical Action*. Oakland, CA: Berrett-Koehler Publishers, 2014.

Bhikhu Parekh. *Gandhi: A Very Short Introduction.* New York, NY: Oxford University Press, 2001.

Srdja Popvic and Matthew Miller. *Blueprint for Revolution: How to Use Rice Pudding, Lego Men, and Other Nonviolence Techniques to Galvanize Communities, Overthrow Dictators, or Simply Change the World.* New York, NY: Spiegel & Grau, 2015.

Bernie Sanders. *Our Revolution: A Future to Believe In.* New York, NY: Thomas Dunne Books, 2016.

Riku Sen. *Stir It Up: Lessons in Community Organizing and Advocacy.* San Francisco, CA: Jossey-Bass, 2003.

Henry David Thoreau. *Civil Disobedience.* CreateSpace Publishing, 2017.

Periodicals and Internet Sources

Paul Danish, "Civil Disobedience in Lafayette and North Dakota," *Boulder Weekly,* January 19, 2017, http://www.boulderweekly.com/opinion/danish-plan/civil-disobedience-in-lafayette-and-north-dakota.

Harold C. Ford, "Remembering the Selma March, the 'Grandest Hour of the Civil Rights Movement,'" *East Village Magazine,* January 17, 2017, http://www.eastvillagemagazine.org/2017/01/17/essay-remembering-the-selma-march-the-grandest-hour-of-the-civil-rights-movement.

Mary Katharine Ham, "Liberals Should Stop Pretending Their Protest Culture Doesn't Hurt People," *The Federalist,* February 3, 2017, http://thefederalist.com/2017/02/03/liberals-should-stop-pretending-bad-behavior-in-their-protest-culture-doesnt-exist-and-hurt-people.

Justin Holcomb, "Report: At Least 180 Federal Workers Planning to Disobey Trump Administration," *Townhall,* February 1, 2017, http://townhall.com/tipsheet/justinholcomb/2017/02/01/report-at-least-180-

federal-workers-planning-how-to-disobey-trump-administration-n2279803.

Matt Kaiser, "Protesting, Civil Disobedience, and Criminal Law," *Above the Law*, February 2, 2017, http://abovethelaw.com/2017/02/protesting-civil-disobedience-and-criminal-law.

Shellie Karabell, "Executive Orders and the Call for Civil Disobedience," *Forbes*, January 31, 2017, http://www.forbes.com/sites/shelliekarabell/2017/01/31/executive-orders-and-the-call-for-civil-disobedience/#2ee29e23de06.

Priyanka Kumar, "What King Learned from Gandhi," *Los Angeles Review of Books*, January 16, 2017, https://lareviewofbooks.org/article/what-king-learned-from-gandhi.

Media for Freedom Staff, "Refusing to Pay Income Taxes for the Trump Agenda," *Media for Freedom*, http://www.mediaforfreedom.com/content/refusing-pay-income-taxes-trump-agenda.

Ben Railton, "The National Park Service and the Legacy of Naturalist Activism," *Huffington Post*, January 25, 2017, http://www.huffingtonpost.com/ben-railton/the-national-park-service_b_14389714.html.

Jannell Ross, "NAACP Chief Promises More Civil Disobedience Against Trump Nominees," *Washington Post*, January 7, 2017, https://www.washingtonpost.com/national/naacp-chief-promises-more-civil-disobedience-against-trump-nominees/2017/01/07/8b528a50-d2b9-11e6-aa0c-f196d8ef0650_story.html.

RT Staff, "Hung Jury in Criminal Case Against Environmental Activist," *RT*, February 3, 2017, https://www.rt.com/usa/376238-trial-mistrial-oregon-climate-change.

Ian Samuel, "What is Wrong with Trump's Immigration Ban? *Al Jazeera*, January 30, 2017, http://www.aljazeera.com/indepth/features/2017/01/wrong-trump-immigration-ban-170130102549929.html.

JC Santos, "Five Things to Keep Yourself Safe During A Civil Disobedience Breakout During A Tour," *Travelers Today*, January 31, 2017, http://www.travelerstoday.com/articles/37007/20170131/five-things-keep-yourself-safe-during-civil-disobedience-breakout-tour.htm.

Lisa Speckhard, "Moving Beyond Marching: Civil Disobedience in the Trump Era," *The Capital Times*, January 25, 2017, http://host.madison.com/ct/news/local/govt-and-politics/moving-beyond-marching-civil-disobedience-in-the-trump-era/article_09bc6428-d887-5813-a91c-25f1a43c54e7.html.

John Williams, "Celebrating Two Centuries of Thoreau," *New York Times*, January 13, 2017, https://www.nytimes.com/2017/01/13/books/review/celebrating-two-centuries-of-thoreau.html.

Index

31901062510336